BE MORE

BONSAI

PENGUIN MICHAEL JOSEPH

UK | USA | Canada | Ireland | Australia
India | New Zealand | South Africa

Penguin Michael Joseph is part of the Penguin Random House group of companies
whose addresses can be found at global.penguinrandomhouse.com

First published by Penguin Michael Joseph, 2022
001
Copyright © Mark Akins and Martin Roach, 2022
Illustrations © Korda Ace
Photographs © Alfie Blue / Harco Visuals
Colour origination by Altaimage, London

The moral right of the author has been asserted

Set in Twentieth Century by Monotype
Typeset by Nathan Burton
Printed and bound in Italy by Printer Trento

The authorized representative in the EEA is Penguin Random House Ireland, Morrison
Chambers, 32 Nassau Street, Dublin D02 YH68

A CIP catalogue record for this book is available from the British Library

ISBN: 978–1–405–95206–4

www.greenpenguin.co.uk

MIX
Paper from
responsible sources
FSC® C018179

Penguin Random House is committed to a
sustainable future for our business, our readers
and our planet. This book is made from Forest
Stewardship Council® certified paper.

BE MORE

BY

MARK AKINS

MICHAEL JOSEPH

CONTENTS

Part 1

THINK ONLY TREE

Most commonly translated as 'tree in a pot', bonsai are intended to be accurate, smaller representations of mature trees seen in nature.

Bonsai also represents a way of life, a calming attitude and serene mentality that can be both hugely rewarding and life-enriching.

'Think only tree.'

With these three words, like so many people before me and indeed since, I started a life-long – and life-changing – love affair with bonsai. It was 1984, and I was watching *The Karate Kid* one evening after school. I loved the film, but more than anything else I was fascinated by the intriguing character of Mr Miyagi, the diminutive, kind and rather eccentric widower who befriends the film's star, seventeen-year-old Daniel LaRusso. As the 'new boy' in school, Daniel was struggling to fit in and had become a target for bullies. I was rooting for him to learn karate and emerge triumphant in the movie's climactic martial arts tournament.

As exciting as those fight scenes were, it was the moment where we first see Mr Miyagi tending to his bonsai that had me completely mesmerized. I had never seen bonsai before or even heard the word, for that matter. Miyagi is seen pruning a juniper while chatting to 'Daniel san'. That scene is a crucial part of the evolution of their friendship, which stretches across age and cultural boundaries.

I was completely captivated.

Shortly afterwards, my grandmother bought me a bonsai seed kit as a surprise gift. The little pack contained a small round terracotta pot, some seeds and a booklet of instructions telling me 'everything' I needed to know. I enthusiastically went through the instructions in my 'read a bit, do a bit' fashion – the seeds got soaked in water and put in the fridge for a while, then taken out and, after a few weeks, I had some seedlings.

Success!

The seedlings lasted a couple of months before they shrivelled up and died.

Undeterred, I eagerly harvested every book I could find about bonsai and spent hour after hour poring over them in my room.

That five-minute scene in *The Karate Kid* had changed my life.

After that, I could, indeed, 'Think only tree.'

It's been a few decades since I had that first bonsai starter seed kit. The art and culture of bonsai has served me well over the years, accompanying me on life's journey and teaching me so much along the way.

Away from the actual horticulture of the bonsai themselves, this obsession has gifted me the most wonderful benefits — bonsai is the one aspect of my life that I have always been able to return to and take refuge in, through both the good and the bad times. Life is not always easy and there are times that I have been glad to take a little solitude and 'think only tree', to exclude the world for a short while and find a little peace. The pace of modern life is so hectic, but for bonsai, there is no rush, no need to compromise priorities, to worry, to forget to practise self-care, to lose perspective, to struggle for balance . . . all these pitfalls and challenges that we face can be brought into sharp focus by the beautiful and ancient art of bonsai.

I now own and run a bonsai nursery, and my passion is to make bonsai accessible to all, promoting the symbiotic relationship between bonsai and wellbeing. Over the years, I have increasingly found significant benefits for my own mental wellbeing and health by learning from the many analogies between bonsai and our lives.

To complement the life lessons we can learn from these magical little trees, you'll also find essential tips and techniques to get you started in this amazing pastime. Hopefully, this will set you on course for a life-long relationship with these miniature works of art.

Of course, I now know that growing a tree from seed is the most difficult way to start bonsai. Those first seedlings from my grandmother might be long since dead, but I do still own the little terracotta pot and I am proud to say that it takes pride of place at my nursery, to serve as a reminder for me of where it all started.

I'm just glad my grandmother didn't get me chopsticks to catch flies with instead.

'Experience the beauties of nature,
and in doing so learn about yourself.'

Japanese proverb

If you hold a bonsai tree in your hand, you are in touch with a story that spans almost two thousand years.

In terms of the origins of bonsai, if you were to ask most people in the street about the history, they would most probably guess that the art form started in Japan. The word 'bonsai' itself is, indeed, Japanese. However, if you are looking for the very first shoots of what we class as bonsai, then it is towards China and its pioneering gardening culture that we must turn our gaze.

Certain scholars suggest that Chinese gardeners were

experimenting with potted trees as far back as two thousand years ago. As a show of how powerful and important these little trees were, numerous Chinese emperors ordered the construction of vast landscaped gardens and lakes that were exact replicas of their expansive real-world kingdoms. Within these bespoke landscapes, the gardens often featured so-called *penjing* – miniature trees in pots. These *penjing* were revered and admired and often formed the central focal point of an imperial garden.

Humans have a long-established fascination with the miniature, with many ancient cave excavations revealing tiny stone or bone carvings and clay figurines, small and portable representations of life-size objects, animals or people. This fascination often extended across numerous cultures into the belief that these miniatures had magical and mystical powers.

Initially, trees that had been 'dwarfed' in nature by the battering of harsh winds, snow, rain and other extreme environments were sourced from the wild and repotted; these trees were often left in nurseries for some time to acclimatize to being at a lower sea level, then potted and displayed in people's homes.

Like its Chinese equivalent, the beginning of the history of bonsai in Japan cannot be given an exact date. Some sources suggest an interest in potted trees and plants as far back as the eighth century; others suggest that travelling Buddhist monks took these 'living sculptures' to Japan in the tenth and eleventh centuries and, quite literally, seeded the art form on their arrival. The hugely revered and lauded Japanese bonsai history is widely regarded as dating to around the early fourteenth century.

Although bonsai on any larger scale did not really take off in the West until the twentieth century, there is evidence of some fourteenth-century European travellers in the Far East taking a few samples of bonsai back home. The first signs that bonsai culture was being exported more widely outside the Far East came around the end of the nineteenth century. There were dwarf trees on display at the Philadelphia Exhibition in 1876, as well as at the Paris Global Exhibition in 1878; Windsor Castle appears to have had some form of a display in 1907, but the first high-profile, large-scale exhibition in England was held in London in 1909. At the time, Edwardian Britain was highly fascinated with ornate and elegant culture, so bonsai was a very appealing new attraction.

The two world wars stunted the growth of bonsai as a popular pastime in the West but, after 1945, there was something of a boom. A Japanese immigrant population was establishing itself around the west coast of the US, and they took bonsai with them. The first ever World Bonsai Convention was held in the 1980s in Japan, and by this point bonsai was a pastime and obsession loved by people all over the world.

Inevitably, bonsai had started to seep into popular culture too, such as film and modern art. Millions of people around the globe cherish their trees as family members. By caring for your own bonsai, you are making your own addition to this history.

These days, perhaps we are less likely to believe that bonsai are literally magical but, nonetheless, if this book and the art of 'being more bonsai' enriches your life and offers you a calmer, more peaceful future, then maybe there is some kind of wonderful alchemy at work.

Part 2

BALANCE

'The best and safest thing is to keep a balance in your life, acknowledge the great powers around us and in us. If you can do that, and live that way, you are really a wise man.'

Euripides

To a bonsai, balance is absolutely crucial.

There are many elements that can put its health in jeopardy if they are imbalanced. The roots support the tree, and the tree supports the roots; any imbalance here could put the tree at risk. Maybe the pot is too small or too big. The branches may be in poor condition; perhaps the soil isn't the correct type or there are too many leaves weighing the branches down. Perhaps the wrong fertilizer has been used. Other factors such as overwatering, pests, disease, the wrong tools — even other people's opinions — can all contribute to whether a bonsai has balance or not. If any imbalance persists for too long, the health of the tree will suffer. Therefore, when we are working on a bonsai, we are always careful not to upset the tree's balance to the point where the tree becomes stressed, damaged or, worse still, begins to die.

Just remember, balance is everything to bonsai.

So it should be to us. Unfortunately, we often don't practise a similar level of care with ourselves.

Balance is vital for a fulfilling, enjoyable and healthy life, yet so many of us feel that we don't have enough — or sometimes any — balance. The pace of modern life is hectic, and it always seems to want to run away with itself.

There is a perceived wisdom that you go through education, get a job at the bottom of a ladder, work your way up as far as you can over several decades, then retire. We all know the derogatory terms for this journey — the 'treadmill', the 'grind', 'the rat race'.

We all want to do well, to strive, to be successful and to

progress. The paradox is that this very aspiration often requires us to do certain things that are at odds with being relaxed, happy and content.

They do not allow us to be balanced.

Perhaps the most obvious area we struggle to find balance in is the notorious 'work–life' balance. Often when we talk about this aspect of modern life, it is in terms of work outweighing life; you rarely hear someone saying, 'Oh, I find I enjoy my life too much. I'm always doing my hobbies, spending time with my loved ones, eating well, having time to relax and enjoy my passions, looking after my physical and mental health . . . I really should slog more at work.'

Think about the most practical demand on a working person's life – the commute: if you commute one hour a day, each way, five days a week, that's ten hours a week. Or almost five hundred hours a year. Assuming that you are awake for, on average, let's say, sixteen hours a day, that means just over one calendar month of your year is spent commuting. This taxing burden is compounded by the financial cost of the commute, but also the cost to your lifestyle and health. I once read that if you commute on a major Underground line for one working year, you inhale a human body's worth of skin and hair!

Often, after an extended break from work, you hear people remark, 'It was actually really nice to step off the treadmill.' This age-old analogy of a treadmill has much value, because at times we all feel as though we are on a treadmill that is just getting quicker and quicker without us even pushing any buttons — and, worse still, sometimes, the faster it goes, the harder it feels to get off. If you feel that your pace of life is moving too fast and you don't have the confidence to step off, then it is all too easy to lose your balance . . . and just as with bonsai, that can have very unhelpful consequences.

Of course, balance can be eroded in every aspect of your life, not just in terms of work. Even if you feel that your work–life balance is acceptable, you may worry that there is an imbalance in your diet, in your health, in your ability to stay calm and not to worry, or perhaps there are key relationships that feel imbalanced. There are also many who feel their financial situation is compromised.

So, what happens when our life does not have balance?

Any bonsai grower's ambition is to tend and nurture a coherent, well-balanced tree with all its component parts working in a fully symbiotic and thriving relationship. If the leaves look glossy and beautiful but, underneath, the roots are squashed and neglected, then those shiny leaves won't be around for long; if the pot is too large and the tree is lost in its surroundings, then it will grow out of proportion and lose its aesthetic balance.

Likewise, if you are succeeding at work but your family life is struggling due to the long hours you are putting in to achieve this, then your wellbeing, and the wellbeing of your family and loved ones, will ultimately deteriorate. Similarly, if you are blessed with a happy home but your work stresses and strains you, then it is inevitable that this negative part of your life will ultimately affect the positive.

So how can you redress the imbalances in your life and enjoy a richer, calmer and more relaxed way forward? Certainly, like bonsai, the first step is to recognize that there is an imbalance, diagnose where it is and decide how you can rectify that problem.

Hopefully, the art of bonsai and the wonderful, calming effect of keeping these little works of art will help you diagnose, assess and remedy your own imbalances so that you can flourish and blossom.

So, if you agree that balance in life is all-important and you want to see how these magnificent miniature trees can help you learn life lessons aplenty, you need to buy yourself a bonsai.

Getting your first bonsai is an exciting time, just like bringing home a puppy . . . albeit without the biting or indoor toileting.

There are a few simple snippets of advice to think about when you are making your first journey into the wonderful world of bonsai – follow these, and you should be able to find a tree that you will be able to care for and love for many years.

1. Set a budget. When you get to a bonsai nursery, you will see trees of all sizes and shapes, which can cost anywhere

from £20 up to £10,000 (or more!). It is easy to get carried away. I have to keep many a secret about buyers who feel they have to creep back into their garden hiding expensive new trees under their arm so as not to let their other half know! Alternatively, nod understandingly when they say, 'I'm looking after this one for a friend!'

2. You should look for a healthy tree with foliage that is vibrant and which has the same colours all over. Look out for obvious warning signs such as a tree that is loose in the pot, broken branches, training wires cutting into the bark or telltale cut marks.

3. Ask questions. You need to be sure the tree will be suitable for the conditions in your garden. A good list would include questions such as:

> When was the tree last repotted, or when will it need repotting?
>
> What fertilizer should I use and how should I apply it?
>
> Should the tree be wired?

How often should I water the tree?

Does the tree prefer full sun or partial shade?

Does it require care beyond what a beginner would know how to give?

Bonsai are not dwarf trees,
nor are they a species of tree.

Good nurseries will welcome questions and encourage you to ask them, both as a future customer and also because that is the bonsai way. You will find that the online bonsai community is super-welcoming of, and helpful towards, beginners.

To return to the puppy analogy, buying a bonsai can be like going to a dog rescue centre – there will be a lot to choose from but, usually, one will stand out more than the others. Go with your heart (provided your heart is within budget!). That will most likely be your tree . . . it is calling out to you.

One of the single biggest misconceptions surrounding bonsai is whether to buy an indoor or an outdoor tree. Essentially, bonsai are outdoor trees, they are grown with that in mind, and the advent of indoor bonsai is a commercial development because people started to want to keep them inside. Many indoor trees, however, are much harder to care for than outdoor trees, and you will need to ensure that the tree gets the correct amount of light, water, heat, humidity and airflow. With both indoor and outdoor bonsai, believe it or not, a tree that has been alive for one hundred years can die in a few days if it isn't looked after properly.

If you are limited by your outdoor space, then I would urge you not to walk away from your first bonsai — just make sure you buy a healthy tree from a choice of species that are more manageable indoors for a beginner, such as a Chinese elm. You could also look out for *Ficus retusa* (fig), *Zanthoxylum piperitum* (Japanese pepper tree) or *Crassula ovata* (jade or money tree).

If you are going to look for an outdoor tree, then your choice widens significantly to include many deciduous, evergreen and coniferous species, all of which should remain outside all year round. Again, some species are easier than others, so I would recommend perhaps *Pinus sylvestris* (Scots pine), *Juniperus chinensis* (Chinese juniper), *Acer palmatum* (Japanese maple) or *Larix kaempferi* (Japanese larch).

One final lesson about bonsai before you go out and welcome your newest potted family member: bonsai trees are designed to be a miniature form of trees found in nature, whether from your local area or trees you have seen on your travels, and although we typically classify them into a category that best describes their physical characteristics, they often may conform to more than one such description.

The widely accepted style categories that you should be aware of are:

Formal upright (*chokkan*)

A somewhat straight, tapering trunk running the length of the tree with an apex formed at the top. For aesthetics, the first branch will start approximately one quarter of the way up the tree, with subsequent and thinner branches alternating around the trunk.

Informal upright (*moyogi*)

A curved, 'S'-shaped trunk that tapers from the base to the top with branches growing from the outside of where the trunk bends.

Cascade (*kengai*)

A tree with one or more branches that overhang the sides of the pot and which grows below the bottom level of the pot. The apex is formed from a small, lower branch. This style is designed to mimic a tree growing on a mountainside and is usually planted in a tall pot.

Cascade (kengai)

Similar in style to a cascade tree, but the tree itself will not grow below the bottom level of the pot. Again, these mimic a tree growing on a mountainside but are planted in a pot that isn't as deep as a cascade style.

A group planting, usually of an odd number of trees, placed in a shallow pot. It's designed to look like a forest setting, so all trees within the group have to play their part in the overall composition and form a single canopy. The trees should be of different thickness to add perspective, with thinner ones at the back.

Raft (*ikadabuki*)

Designed to look like a tree that has fallen on its side; the branches then grow as separate trunks. These individual trunks will be connected by the old trunk, which remains visible below the new canopy.

Root over rock (*seki-joju*)

As the name suggests, the roots of the tree are grown over a rock before entering the pot. Designed to mimic a tree growing over a rocky area, where the soil has been eroded over time.

Multi-trunk (*kabudachi*)

This is a single tree with multiple trunks growing from a single root. The trunks will usually be of differing thicknesses and combine to form a single canopy, sometimes staggered.

A depiction of a tree growing in a position that is battered by wind, usually from one direction. The trunk will slant slightly in the direction that the wind blows, as will all of the branches.

A style that mimics a tree growing in a densely packed area so its best chance of surviving is to grow tall with all foliage mainly at the top. They sometimes display a crooked trunk with added deadwood features, adding to their story.

Semi-cascade (han-kengai)

Buying your first bonsai is an exciting and invigorating new experience. Armed with these tips, you should be able to find a miniature companion in life that will remain healthy, feel hugely rewarding and will undoubtedly make a significant difference to your life.

SO, CHOOSE WISELY . . . AND WELCOME TO THE WORLD OF BONSAI!

In 1976, Japan presented America with fifty-three priceless bonsai trees and six viewing stones to celebrate the USA's bicentennial.

YOU AND YOUR TREE

'Take care of your body.
It's the only place you have to live.'

Jim Rohn, author, speaker
and entrepreneur

Every part of a bonsai is vital to its health and wellbeing, but the trunk and branches are, without doubt, essential for the tree to enjoy a long and happy life. Circumstances around the trunk and branches may change — the leaves may come and go, the soil can be swapped, the pot might be altered — but the trunk remains the key structural component, providing stability to everything that you see. The health of the trunk is the result of a combination of many elements — the pot, the soil, the nutrients the tree receives, pests — and if these are not kept in balance, then the tree itself may fail.

The trunk has to be prioritized.

Our own trunk – the body – can all too frequently be neglected, a result of the pressures of modern life. How many of us have put our health on hold to complete an 'important' project, or compromised our diet in order to 'get the job done'? Have you ever become so busy with work that your exercise or hobbies fall by the wayside? Just like a bonsai, unless we care for the trunk and prioritize our health, we risk everything. If the trunk fails, then it is game over, just as it will be if we neglect our bodies.

You can't say to a bonsai, 'I am busy right now, I will look after you in a few weeks when this crazy work project is completed.'

Simply put, the tree would die.

You cannot allow that to happen to a bonsai.

Nor should you allow that to happen to yourself.

There is a vital truth here to be learned from the importance of caring for a bonsai's trunk that also applies to caring for ourselves:

If it is snowing, or very windy, or freezing,
or there is torrential rain . . .

. . . *those* are the times when you should
be *more* attentive to bonsai, not less.

When trees are stressed and under demands that may threaten their wellbeing, that is when we must be more attentive. Similarly, it is precisely when life becomes more demanding that we have to be kinder to ourselves, not less.

So, next time you are 'up against it' with a project, realize that this is the time to prioritize your health and physical wellbeing. After all, how do you expect to do your best work if you aren't eating properly, drinking enough water, exercising or taking time out to relax while under extra pressure?

In the longer term, you need to recognize that repeatedly putting your 'trunk' and physical health second (or third or fourth or . . .) will lead to health problems.

It would be unrealistic to expect a bonsai to win a competition if you haven't looked after that tree for weeks or months. If you don't water the tree properly, then guess what? It will be dehydrated and suffer. If you don't apply quality 'food' to that tree, then it will become dull and jaded. If you do this for weeks on end, neglecting the tree right at the time when it needed you the most, would you then be surprised if it wilted and maybe even died?

No. So do not treat yourself any differently.

It's important to take some time to plan out how and when you can reliably prioritize your health during any busy period. We all know the benefits of healthy eating, exercise and hydration, but so often these are overlooked when times are challenging. What bonsai teaches us is that the health of your trunk – and, by association, everything in your life – is always more important than your career, your bank balance or your popularity.

Taking care of your trunk needn't be complicated. When you know you have an intense period approaching, don't just plunge into the chaos without first thinking about what you are going to be eating, as well as when and how you are going to access that food.

Apply the same care to other areas of your life that impact on your 'trunk'. Look at the week ahead and think of how and when you can exercise or enjoy your hobbies. Sitting at your desk for hours on end is a known cardiovascular and high-blood-pressure risk, so break up that inactivity with a gentle stroll, which is both healthy for your trunk and refreshing for your mind. Always be determined to get moving, but especially during times of strain. If you can, aim to water your trunk correctly – the recommended amount of water to drink each day is eight glasses – and no, alcohol isn't classed as watering!

Just as every bonsai tree is individual, so are the ways in which we maintain a healthy body. What works for one person may not necessarily work for another. Be objective, be caring towards yourself and, if something doesn't contribute to the health of your 'trunk', then change it. Learn to know when your 'trunk' needs particular attention and realize that doing this will lead to a better outcome in all areas of your life.

Finally, as with all things bonsai, don't forget balance. Eating better doesn't mean a restricted diet, nor does it mean only eating things that you don't like. It doesn't dictate that you should never have a glass of red wine if you enjoy that. Whether you are under extra pressure or just trundling along through a quiet spell, always allow yourself treats; otherwise, caring for your trunk can become a dull, uphill battle.

In *Home Alone 2*, while serving ice cream to Macaulay Culkin's character Kevin McCallister, a hotel porter asks the young boy, 'Two scoops, sir?' To which Kevin replies, 'Two . . . make it three, I'm not driving.'

So, when you work hard to keep your trunk healthy, don't be afraid to occasionally leave your keys at home and go for three scoops every now and again.

'Our bodies are our gardens, to the which our wills are gardeners.'

WILLIAM SHAKESPEARE

*'The wise man does not lay up his own
treasures. The more he gives to others,
the more he has for his own.'*

Every autumn, a deciduous tree will shed its leaves. They turn
a beautiful array of yellows, oranges, reds and browns . . .
then blow gently away in the wind.

From the tree's perspective, those leaves have served their
purpose, brought energy and joy and the time has come to
let them go. Those leaves will go on to provide joy and
purpose elsewhere. As children, we all loved making a pile
of leaves to jump into, collecting a few to put into scrapbooks
or scooping up big handfuls for the compost heap; even now,

as a 'proper grown-up', I still love crunching across a woodland floor coated in crisp, autumn leaves. Each and every dropped leaf continues to serve a purpose beyond the needs of the tree upon which it originally grew: small animals use them for making nests; insects and a whole host of bacteria and fungi feed on them and break them down for other microbial life to feast upon; some bat species snuggle up in the leaves and would not survive a cold winter without them.

Much like the leaves of a tree, we often gather possessions around us and feel some degree of satisfaction from owning more and more. Yet sometimes those 'leaves' can cause our branches to begin to sag. More possessions lead to the need for more storage; the more we collect, the more we need to dust, the more we need to maintain . . . and so the canopy of our 'leaves' gets ever bigger.

However, unlike trees, we don't always let our 'leaves' go when they no longer fulfil their purpose. But how can we expect to find balance if our canopy of leaves is buckling under its own weight?

When my wife, Sally, was pregnant, we moved into a four-bedroom house with a garage, having lived in a nice one-bedroom flat. Our possessions immediately looked lost in the larger house. Twenty years later, and that bigger house is now crammed, the garage is full of all sorts and my car has never ever been in there! . . . Sound familiar?

The turning point for me was back in 2011, when, unfortunately, our home was burgled. As well as the usual assorted electronics that were stolen, the thieves also took items with much more sentimental value, things that had been passed down through the family and were of little or no value to anyone else – they even stole my wedding cufflinks.

I was far more bothered by those sentimental items than the fact that someone had been in our home. Sally reacted differently and didn't feel safe for quite some time.

The way I came to view that incident was this: the burglary had happened, I couldn't impact or control that fact, but what I could control was my response to it. My conclusion was that 'things are just things'.

Those items were just leaves.

For me, bonsai dropping their leaves showed me that the answer was some level of minimalism. I am not radical in getting rid of things, I don't live in an empty box, but I do like to dispose of things that I no longer need or want.

So, if your life is feeling cluttered, think about dropping some leaves.

When thinking about dropping some leaves, ask yourself these simple questions:

Does this item bring me joy?

Do I expect to use this item in the next twelve months?

Is this item hard to get hold of?

Do I really need this item?

If the answer to any of the above is 'yes', then the item should be kept. If you are unable to answer 'yes' to any of these questions, then it is time to 'drop that leaf'.

You could start small, with a drawer or a cupboard, for example, and work your way up to sorting out whole rooms. The exercise itself feeds the desire to get through the task

and, just like a tree, we end up with just the essential items that make us happy. Think of whether you will get rid of the items in question, pass them on or give them a new life. Just like those leaves that were dropped by the tree and made compost or kept that bat from feeling the cold, your unwanted possessions can help others.

There are many options for unwanted items – for example, you could give them away or donate them to charity. Take satisfaction in knowing that they will bring joy to someone else – their journey does not end once you part with the item.

If you have any clothing that no longer fits you or suits your wardrobe, give it to a charity shop. That way, the charity in question gets some income when they sell the items, and the clothes can go on to give the new owner joy and benefit long after they would have just sat gathering dust in your wardrobe.

Here's another example of a way in which you could drop your leaves. A number of years ago I purchased a classic car from 1975 with the aim of restoring it. All went well for a while, but, as I became more and more busy with work, I couldn't find time for the restoration and the car sat untouched under a cover for over twelve months. Eventually, I realized that if I held on to the car any longer, it was going to rot beyond repair, which would be both a waste and a great shame. So I chose to give the car away to a local family. This could have been a difficult decision, but the joy I could see in the family made my mind up very quickly. The car got a new lease of life and the family thoroughly enjoyed getting 'Myrtle' – as they named her – back on the road.

If the 'leaves' you wish to drop are too valuable to give away or donate, then you are, of course, at liberty to sell them. That said, if I die before my wife, I just hope she doesn't sell my trees for what I told her I paid for them!

Once you start the process of regularly dropping leaves, it does become easier. It's much like displaying bonsai trees – each tree should have elbow room to be appreciated and seen, rather than crammed in, struggling for space.

Of course, it's no good dropping a few leaves if we then go out and replace the items with new ones! Our society is so centred on consumerism and, of course, many people regard that as a great bonus for economic, social and other reasons. However, as tempting as the 'Sales' and bargains are, as easy as it is to go on your phone and buy something with your thumbprint or a single click, next time you find yourself loitering around a clothing rail or hovering over a 'Buy Now' button, pause and ask yourself: 'Do I need to buy this item today or can I ask myself again next month?'

Very often, this one simple question is all it takes to help control impulsive buying urges.

After all, we all have our weaknesses. You might not be that surprised to find out that I collect bonsai pots. Some will get used, and some won't. I quite like the chatter I get from them as they sit on display in readiness for the right tree. However, if someone spots a bonsai pot that is ideal for one of their trees, then I will let that pot go so that it can continue spreading joy.

You can do this all year round or all at once — it's entirely up to you. We've all heard of a spring clean, well, why not have a clear-out around October/November and call it your 'Autumn Leaf Drop'?

Dropping our leaves doesn't mean living in an empty house with only a single cup, plate, one knife and fork and a few basic items of clothing to wear. There should always be a balance to life, and possessions are part of that mix. However, don't be afraid to let go of possessions that do not add any intrinsic value to your life. That value could either be a capability, a function or purely joy, but if an object satisfies none of these objectives, then let it go.

The added bonus of dropping your leaves regularly is that, once you have shed your unwanted items, moving forward will be so much easier – pruning and styling a bonsai that has lost its leaves is much simpler and more enjoyable, because there are no distractions and no unnecessary foliage in the way.

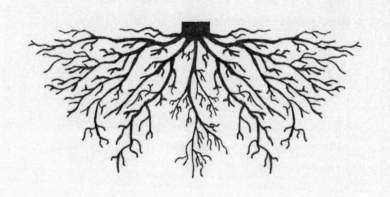

'Be not afraid of growing slowly,
be afraid only of standing still.'

The roots of a bonsai perform two functions. The first is to gather water, air and nutrients so that the tree can continue to grow, develop and show itself off when flowering. The second is to anchor the tree into the soil, giving it support when nature throws its force against it. There are two types of root: thick, hardened ones that serve little purpose, clog up the soil and prevent water from draining; and sinuous, fibrous ones that nourish and support the tree, allowing it to thrive.

The workings of the roots and the upper parts of any tree, not just a bonsai, have to be in sync: the roots support the tree, and the tree supports the roots. As I mentioned earlier, imbalance can put everything in jeopardy.

Luckily, bonsai roots can be modified, altered and reappraised. The bonsai can be removed from its pot, the roots trimmed and then the tree repotted to encourage a fresh surge of growth.

Our own beliefs and ethics are no different – they are what support us, they make us who we are, they are the core of everything about us. Everyone holds their own individual set of beliefs and ethics, just as each bonsai has a unique set of roots. These will distinguish what we consider to be proper behaviour and what we consider to be improper. We are anchored by these ideas; some stay with us our entire lives, others alter over time. They help to shape what we become.

Like the flexible, sinuous roots of a healthy bonsai, light, generous and considerate beliefs and ethics are inclusive and fill your life – and the lives of those around you – with positivity. Similarly, just like the hard, inflexible roots of some trees, negative beliefs and ethics are more likely to be divisive and cloud your mind and life with negativity.

Living a life that is full of hardened, stubborn roots will mean that you are unable to be inquisitive, open and generous — essentially remaining narrow-minded. By contrast, if we encourage thirsty, fibrous roots that shoot out into our environment to take in nourishment, new thoughts and fresh ideas, then we can remain hungry to evolve, to learn and to grow.

If your beliefs and ethics — your roots — are not looking to remain fresh, then your life will never be enriched.

Just like a bonsai, it is possible for you to examine and then change your beliefs; they are not made of stone. When we look to make changes, it is behaviour that is most evident to us, so this is where we should begin. We have the ability to evaluate our own behaviour every day, at work, at home, when driving, when we are out and about, or even when we simply have time alone. There is often a thin line between getting things right and getting things wrong, and our behaviour can often hinge on a split-second turning point. If you do regret things afterwards, you have the immediate opportunity to add a new fibrous root — a new behaviour — which is to say sorry and apologize. This is not a weakness but a moment to put things right and move on.

Re-evaluate your roots, your beliefs and ethics regularly and you will find that in certain areas of your life you start to gradually change your approach towards everyday situations and the people around you. The way in which we think about the world is very personal, and we cannot influence the beliefs and ethics of others, but each of us can analyse and evolve the way in which we behave.

Many people consider it (a tree known as *Goshin* - "Protector of the Spirits") to be the most famous bonsai in the world. This spectacular tree was created by the legendary John Naka, and combines eleven separate junipers, one for each of his eleven grandchildren.

It takes strength to be honest with yourself through regular self-examination, to not only analyse what you consider to be proper and improper but to actually make a change afterwards. Are you prepared to debate your beliefs rationally and calmly with others? You should not be forced or coerced into accepting others' beliefs, and neither should you force your beliefs on others. You should always look to form a balanced and considered view, even if it is ultimately at odds with your initial view.

Always be open to growth, to new roots and to an open mind.

This idea is one that lasts throughout your life. A bonsai tree does not stagnate in early adulthood but continues to evolve and grow during its entire life, regardless of age. It sends out new sinuous roots to find new food, just as an open mind can still be learning and feeding the brain for the whole of a person's life.

So, just like your bonsai, you should inspect your roots often, and be open to new ideas and growth . . . always. Let the sinuous, flexible, nourishing roots flourish.

What do you want to be? Narrow-minded? Or expansive and inquisitive?

THE POT (FAMILY)

'There are only two ways to live your life:
one is as though nothing is a miracle.
The other is as if everything is.'

A bonsai pot forms a barrier between the tree and the outside world. Everything inside the pot will contribute to what its life becomes. Some pots are unglazed, some are glazed, some come in fancy colours or with ornate decoration, some are very shallow. And yes, some pots are more blingy than others, just like us!

The key is to marry the pot with each individual tree so the combination is balanced and mutually beneficial. If a tree sits in an ill-fitting pot, then it will never have a fulfilling life. A pot that is too small will damage the roots; the drainage will become poor and water won't flow properly through the soil. If a bonsai is placed in a pot that is too big, it will quickly grow out of shape and the aesthetics of the tree will be lost.

The choice of pot should be decided by assessing what is ultimately good for the tree.

Your life should be no different.

There are multiple elements that go into your pot and your life, but to get you started with this idea, let's look at the most obvious example – our homes. These are our private spaces, where we have all our possessions: practical items, sentimental objects, memories, unwanted or unused clutter . . . everything. Some people's pots are larger than others, some are more colourful and extrovert, some are more minimal. But we can all acknowledge the truth that what we decide to put into that pot will materially affect our lives.

At this point, it is worth mentioning social media – which, unfortunately, seems to prompt many people to either boast about their 'pot' or at least make their pot look far more impressive than it actually is. Our lives are a little more complicated than a simple social media page – by this I mean that we have an internal and an external image, but those two components may not always necessarily have a clean meeting place. Here, you need to start thinking honestly about yourself and – whether you like the answer or not – it becomes a starting point and something that you can work with.

With regards to change, the bonsai pot also mimics life in the natural sequence of growing bigger and bigger before being downsized. People move into their first property, then perhaps they have kids, the family grows – there often evolves a need for a bigger property; eventually, it is likely that the family will shrink as time goes by, the house will become quieter and people then have the opportunity to look at downsizing (in turn, our own 'saplings' may well seek their own first pot).

A tree moving into its first real bonsai pot may also feel like its forever home; however, this is just the beginning. It will have many pots to come, and the pot may have many trees to house. People often dislike the idea of moving house because their home understandably holds lots of memories of happy times. The reality is that these memories are all in our heads, as well as in photos and videos, and we can carry these with us throughout life. Your old home will provide another family with shelter and room to grow, making their own memories, just as it did for you.

Just as a bonsai can suffer if it is placed in a pot that is too large, similarly, if you live in a home that is too big — essentially living beyond your means — then that can cause problems. Your bills may become overwhelming and start to create stress and pressure on your finances, when in fact your home should only be a source of happiness.

There are other times when a pot needs to be changed — sometimes life may cause a pot to get cracked. Maybe someone accidentally knocks a bonsai over, or it is damaged by harsh weather or — very often — a family pet. Some people discard the pot because it is not 'perfect'; however, in true bonsai culture, the cracks are often celebrated through the art of *kintsugi*, where a vivid glue is used to immortalize the damage, which is regarded as a part of the tree's story and therefore celebrated, rather than hidden away.

Maybe your own 'pot' has been too compressed or stressed and an incident or series of events has caused a problem or a 'crack'? When this happens, if circumstances allow, your own pot doesn't necessarily need to be changed or discarded. As long as you maintain a balance between what your pot can accommodate and what is right for you, then these smaller changes can be hugely beneficial.

In bonsai culture, there is a rule of thumb that the length of the pot should be two thirds the height of the tree; by similarly tailoring your life to your circumstances, you can achieve a much healthier and more fulfilling balance.

There are often times when we naturally stop and analyse our 'pot'. For example, at the beginning of each new year people often give good thought to the direction of their life; other people reflect on such things during their annual holiday. Whatever the motivation, it is a healthy habit to look at your pot regularly and honestly then ask yourself some simple questions. For example:

Is this pot still right for my life?

How feasible is it to change pots?

Is it the pot that is causing problems, or other factors?

Will those same factors still be there when I have changed pots?

The trick is to view repotting as an entirely positive experience — one that is being done to make your life easier, more enjoyable and happier. You are being brave and wise enough to look at your pot, assess what it needs and change to suit those demands.

After all, the perfect pot will enable a tree to become healthy, vibrant and happy with its life.

So, be brave.

Assess your pot.

Take what action you can afford and find your own perfect pot.

Personally, I do not hold any sentimental value in bricks and mortar. There will come a time when I know I need to change my pot and, as part of that, I will look to find a property that is adequately scaled to suit my life moving forward.

Maybe a nice two-bedroom bungalow, somewhere quiet. It would have to have a reasonably sized but not fussy garden for my bonsai trees . . . and a seat in the sun.

I am looking forward to the change.

At that moment, my pot will be perfectly suited to the tree.

There are a number of factors to consider when buying a pot. The pot should reflect the tree's characteristics. Is it tall, slender, short, squat or curvy? Does it have lots of twists, deadwood or a delicate canopy? Does the pot have curved edges, straight edges, delicate feet or maybe even some decoration? These are all considerations to throw into the mix.

A standard pot can be round, oval, square or rectangular and is typically shallow. This style of pot would usually be paired with an upright style of tree. The guidance here is that the length of the pot should be around two thirds of the height of the tree above the pot.

A semi-cascade pot will be as tall as it is wide, and more often than not square, round or hexagonal. The tree to suit it would be a semi-cascade style where the lower branch of the tree dips or hangs below the top of the pot, but not lower than the bottom of the pot.

A cascade pot will usually be taller than its width and is often square, round or hexagonal to accommodate a cascade-style tree, which will have a lower branch that dips or hangs below the bottom of the pot.

There are several other styles of pots available, such as crescent pots (resembling a crescent moon), *nanban* pots (round with an irregular edge), and other free-form pots made by artisan potters.

A final word on pot glazes: from a purely aesthetic point of view, a coniferous tree should go into an unglazed pot. This allows the tree to be the main focus, with little to focus attention away from it. Glazed pots are almost exclusively used for deciduous and flowering trees.

With regards to pots, above all else make sure you choose one that is right for your tree and that also appeals to you.

Repotting a bonsai tree can be a stressful activity, not least for the tree. Let's start by defining repotting versus what is known as 'slip-potting'.

Repotting describes how a tree is fully extracted from the pot, removing the old soil and a proportion of the roots. The tree is then put back into the same pot or a new one, according to aesthetic requirements.

Slip-potting refers to simply taking the tree out of its current pot, placing it into a larger pot and filling the gaps with additional soil. This allows the tree to continue growing in line with the intended design. This also serves as an emergency option if the pot is broken or smashed.

The first reason is purely health-related — when the tree becomes 'pot bound', that is, in too small a pot, the roots have no more space to grow.

The second reason is as part of a design change or progression, when we might also choose to completely change the angle at which the tree sits in relation to the pot.

The third and final reason is a broken or damaged pot, which can be remedied with either a slip-potting of the tree or a standard repotting, if the time of year allows.

When to repot

The standard advice is to repot bonsai trees in spring, when new growth appears and new buds are about to burst into leaf, but there are some exceptions.

The first consideration is that spring usually arrives sometime in April. The second consideration is that not all trees wake up in spring at the same rate and therefore the period of repotting could be spaced out over a month or so.

Plan your repotting activity over winter, identify the pot and obtain the other materials you will need, such as soil, wire and pot mesh in readiness.

The generally accepted steps to follow are:

1. Cut any wires that are holding the tree in the pot from underneath and remove the tree.

2. Remove old soil from around the roots using a chopstick, root hook or root rake. You can then trim the roots, but do not remove more than 30 per cent of the root mass. Remove as much of the old soil as is practicable, but do not remove too much root.

3. Offer the tree into the pot, noting that there should ideally be around 25mm around the root ball and underneath. It may be necessary to remove more roots or consider a larger pot if this is not achievable.

4. Prepare the new pot by securing pot mesh over the drainage holes and running the holding wires in readiness.

5. Mound soil into a heap in the centre of the pot, put the tree in at the correct angle, then wriggle the tree down to ensure the soil is evenly spread underneath. Wrap

the holding wires over the tree's root ball and lightly fasten them to hold the tree in position.

6. Fill the remaining space with soil, using a chopstick to ensure the soil fills all gaps, before tightening the holding wires and cutting off any excess length. You can then dress the soil surface with a gravel, pure akadama (bonsai soil) or moss for a more decorative finish, if desired.

Repotting aftercare

Your tree's repotting aftercare may well mean the difference between life and death for the tree. As you can imagine, the repotting process will put stress on the tree, so it is essential that we provide the right environment for it to recover.

For two or three weeks after the repotting, place the tree in a slightly shaded and sheltered location, and do not undertake major foliage pruning during the same growing period, as this will only increase stress on the tree.

You can use root-promoting products that can be added to the watering or applied as a foliage spray, but do not apply a high-nitrogen fertilizer during this time.

Once you are accustomed and comfortable with repotting, your trees stand a much better chance of thriving and moving forward in life. Much like you!

'It's easier to act your way into a new way of thinking than it is to think your way into a new way of acting.'

A bonsai's routine is based around the seasons, putting out new growth in response to rising temperatures and increasing daylight hours, then slowing down in response to reducing temperatures and shorter daylight hours. The bonsai responds according to these changes, safe in the knowledge that a simple routine and preparation works best.

The bonsai doesn't need to think, it simply acts!

We can liken our routines and habits to the soil that a bonsai tree grows in. The soil is what the tree lives in, and its ingredients make up the bonsai's everyday life. The trunk, roots and leaves all exist around the soil but, without the latter, none of the other elements would survive. If the soil is not a healthy environment, then the tree will not thrive, but rather bimble along growing poorly (or not at all) and getting ever weaker. Likewise, if the soil isn't regularly refreshed and kept in tip-top condition, the tree will definitely not stay healthy.

The concepts of routines and habits are so instrumental to our lives in terms of balance and joy. They can allow us to thrive but, if not carefully managed, can slowly drag us down. So, just like bonsai soil, we need to find the right mix of routines and habits to enable us to get the most out of life. Sometimes that might include changing a routine or habit – a part of our 'soil' – so that we can move forward.

A routine is a system or series of actions that serve some function in your life. Some of our routines are relatively passive, in the sense that we do them every day, like a commute. Some are more active, where we perhaps go for a run or work out at the gym a few times a week. Either type requires thought and effort. Having certain set routines makes unimportant parts of our days easy, allowing headspace for the things that need more focus.

Habits are generally considered to be routines of choice that become ingrained and almost unconscious — one rule of thumb suggests that if you perform a routine for thirty consecutive days, it will become a habit. Habits are not inherently negative — always eating five fruit and veg a day can only be a good thing. Obviously, there are other habits that are less helpful.

Just as changing the soil in your bonsai's pot will lead to a flush of vibrancy in your tree, you can change the routines and habits in your life and feel significant benefits. And just as with your bonsai's soil, every now and again it's good to look at our routines objectively and ask if there is an opportunity to mix it up a little. Change can often ignite a great leap forward.

One of my good friends, Matt, is a professional bodybuilder and coach. His weight, body fat and muscle mass will fluctuate depending on whether he is competing or not. He will then have a recovery period, post-competition. All of this is based strictly around very precise routines and habits (plus an enormous amount of discipline, of course).

With this in mind, here is an approach to establishing new routines and habits that I find often works – although I'm not going to lie, on more than one occasion I have found myself in McDonald's only a few days into a 'new routine' of healthy eating. (In my defence, sometimes it is healthy for you to acknowledge those slip-ups – we are all human. Plus. Big Macs taste so good. Don't tell Matt.)

Assuming you want to change an element of your 'soil' in some way, here's one way to do what I like to call a 'Soil Switch'.

Write down what you would like an average week to look like in terms of routines and habits, including as many specific details as you can: what time you would like to wake up, everything you would like to do in your day, mealtimes, who you would like to spend time with, when you prefer to watch your favourite programmes, and what time you would like to go to bed. Put down a full week's worth.

This will take a little time, but it is a wise investment, because writing it down will both cement the ideas in your head and act as a helpful reminder of the new plan.

Once the first week is over, think back over the last seven days and see what you were able to do. If there are items on the list that you didn't manage to do, don't scold yourself — there is no failure here — just think about what changes need to be made the following week to improve and move forward. Maybe you didn't schedule enough time to cook a meal one night and ended up eating convenience food? Maybe you worked too late and were too tired to go to the gym?

Be honest, but be gentle with yourself. This is not about forcing your life and yourself into a new direction. Throughout the following weeks or months of this soil switch, you should remember the following things.

- Habits can take some time to form, so do not pause or give up; be as patient as your bonsai. Stay focused and remain positive with yourself.

- Avoid distractions that will get in the way of the desired new habit. For example, the snooze button on your alarm, the sweets at the till when you stop off for petrol on the way to the gym or the smell of the fast food when you walk past.

- Set yourself up to succeed. If you struggle to exercise first thing in the morning, schedule a gym visit in the early evening. If you hate swimming, don't suddenly set yourself fifty lengths a day as your new goal. Give yourself every chance to succeed.

- Surround yourself with people who can, and will, support you in the changes you would like to make.

Stay patient, stay bonsai, and you will find that your soil switch creates new habits that enable you to have a healthier, more balanced life with greater benefits to you and those around you.

Procrastinating will not make this happen any more than thinking about changing your bonsai's soil will help your tree; you need to start taking action. We will never change our habits if we only think about changing them. You have to make things happen, and it's better to make them happen slowly, rather than not at all.

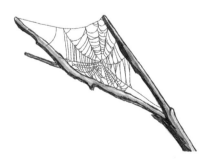

No word of a lie, if I asked fifty bonsai artists what soil to use, I would get fifty different answers!

When it comes to life inside the pot, your choice of soil and how it is prepared is the most important factor. At a basic level, tree roots need water and air.

Bonsai trees can suffer from over- and under-watering. Therefore, the soil needs a water-retentive component that will hold water when available but then release it for the roots to take up. In bonsai, this is typically a clay material known as akadama, but alternatives include compost, bark chippings and sphagnum moss, among others.

When we consider bonsai soil, the air resides between the gaps in the soil and is taken up by fine feeder roots. If your soil is too compacted or waterlogged, then there will be no gaps, the roots will drown and you will get root rot. Free-draining components tend to be inorganic in nature, such as pumice, stone or similar substitutes.

Let's now take a quick look at why the possible fifty answers about soil are all valid in their own right. Depending on where in the world a bonsai tree is growing, weather conditions and climate factors can also affect the soil. A tree in a warmer climate will need watering more often and so more water-retentive components should be added. A tree growing in a wetter climate will require less water-retentive ability and would favour a free-draining soil, particularly during the colder months. This even applies on a macro-level, where two trees on the same street might have very different requirements, depending on whether they are north- or south-facing.

You may therefore need to proceed with a little trial and error to get the best soil mix for your bonsai's environment. Persevere — your trees will thank you for it!

THE OUTSIDE WORLD

'If a problem can be solved, then it's not worth worrying about; if it can't be solved, then it's useless to worry about it.'

Water is the single most important element in looking after your bonsai. Without correct watering, a tree that has been alive for centuries might be dead in days.

Water is an amazing substance: it brings life and supports every living thing on the planet, yet it is transparent, odourless, tasteless, calorie-free — and the water on our earth today is the same water that's been here for nearly 5 billion years. In theory, the water you drink from your glass is the very same that the dinosaurs were gulping down 65 million years ago. It is soft, yet it can wear down the hardest of rock. It can completely fill the biggest cavern yet slip through the smallest of gaps. It follows its own natural path, flowing around objects or, if it so chooses, smashing things out of its way.

Whatever the circumstances,
water continues on its own path.

In simple terms, we pour water on to the soil surface to allow the roots to take up some of the liquid that is eventually transpired through the leaves. Just as your bonsai is enriched and kept healthy by water, in life we would do well to follow water's lead, specifically in four areas of our lives.

First, understand that when water travels through the soil and roots of a bonsai, the tree does not resist or fight to get more water nor try to alter its path. Likewise, in life, we should accept that we cannot control every aspect of our daily experiences that passes us by. Sometimes things will happen that we just have to accept. The urge to always be in control risks putting a lot of stress and pressure on us. Of course, we want to be in charge of our own lives, to look after ourselves, our family and our career, but it isn't realistic to expect to control everything.

While you cannot necessarily control what life throws at you, you can control the way you react to those events. People tend to find the idea of not controlling their future quite worrying and stressful, because they don't know where life is taking them. Take lessons from water and learn to 'go with the flow'. Water flows as it always does, yet it does not know its destination, and when it reaches an obstacle it has the ability to deal with that, then carry on its journey.

The second lesson is that water always takes the path of least resistance. People often say that I am laid-back . . . but the truth is that it takes effort to appear effortless, although, eventually, being effortless is effortless!

This is a mental state, not a physical one, and it can mean adjusting your view, expectations and hopes to allow the path of least resistance to be yours. Don't confuse this idea with laziness; instead, you are just expending the least amount of energy to achieve something.

Ask yourself this: why would you choose the path of most resistance?

Imagine you have fallen into a fast-flowing river and are clinging to a rock, straining against the current, scrabbling around to find a way out – very quickly you will grow tired and, unless you are rescued, you will become exhausted and possibly drown.

However, if you choose to bob along, going with the flow, you will keep your head above water and, with a little luck, find the occasional log to cling on to.

Life is certainly a fast-flowing river, and the things that we cling on to might be a job, a business, a relationship, or just a pair of old boots. Clinging on to these things when they no longer work in your favour is prolonging the inevitable, causing you distress. The sooner you deal with the issue, the better it will be for you. It is also worth remembering that you might not always have to 'let go' – merely 'loosening your grip' may be sufficient.

Equally, you might also be resisting something that could work out to be in your favour. I was once asked to move my family from our rural base to a city in order to continue working for a certain organization. After much deliberation, I decided to let this opportunity pass and to go with the flow. It was a hard decision to make, but it is one that has certainly worked out for the best. I suspect that I would not own a bonsai nursery, or have even written this book, if I had chosen differently.

If you think about it, following the path of least resistance has never stopped water going where it needs to go. Just look at the Grand Canyon!

Make your life simple.

Water also teaches us a third lesson: if there is a problem in life, it is better to confront the issue early on, before the trickle becomes a torrent. Most major rivers start with a small stream that gradually grows bigger and bigger. When rainfall running off hills and mountains is added, the river suddenly has the potential to break its banks.

We all have a number of 'streams' flowing in our life, but the trick is to deal with them early, while they are small and fairly insignificant. If you have a minor disagreement, it is easier to talk it over and make up straight away, rather than let it drag on and become a raging current.

A simple example would be parking tickets. We all know how easy it is to get wound up about them. While we may not like having to pay them, you are much better off dealing with it and moving on, which quickly releases the issue mentally from your mind.

Finally, we would do well to mimic water's ability to always return to a calm, balanced state. When possible, any expanse of water will naturally be calm, unless external factors are causing winds, currents, waterfalls, and so on. When a pebble is thrown into a lake, it will create a splash and ripples will emanate across the surface. Then, before long, the water will return to its still, resting state.

I like to think of this image when I need to calm my mind back to still water.

That is how we should all aspire to be.

Completely calm, with not even a ripple.

The smallest bonsai category is
mame, which translates as 'bean',
and comprises trees that are between
one and three inches tall.

Watering your bonsai is the most difficult task to get right, yet it is also the most crucial: too much water and a tree can drown; too little and the tree simply shrivels up and dies.

There are a couple of ways to tell if a bonsai needs watering. One of the simplest is that the colour changes in the soil at the surface or just underneath. Another way is to push a chopstick into the soil to see if the wood changes colour where it absorbs moisture. Another reliable method is picking up the bonsai to gauge its weight. A watered bonsai with its wet soil is always heavier than a bonsai with dry soil.

Sensing if your tree needs water becomes almost intuitive after a while. There is no simple single answer as to how often a tree needs to be watered, but there are three factors that impact the frequency that you will need to observe:

1. Species of tree

Some trees like very little water and some like to sit in water. You will need to research your species and find the specific answer for the bonsai you have.

2. Soil mix

If you have a good, free-draining soil mix, then you will need to water more often than if you have a water-retentive mix.

3. Aspect

A bonsai tree situated in full sun will need to be watered more often than a tree in partial shade. More sun, and therefore heat, will cause the tree to transpire more to keep cool and the soil itself will dry out through evaporation.

These three factors combined will determine how quickly the soil dries out, and, with this in mind, you can tailor your soil mix and aspect in order to reduce the frequency of watering.

When you water your trees, make sure that you water them thoroughly. A light watering will most likely not make the soil wet throughout and the bottom part of the pot will remain dry. If you are unsure, stand your trees in a trough of water for ten minutes before returning them to their usual location.

Likewise, do not assume that you don't need to water your bonsai if it has been raining. A light drizzle may not make it past the tree canopy, let alone through the soil.

During the winter, there is less need to water trees — in fact, it is more likely that we need to protect our bonsai from too much water. Deciduous trees will not transpire water through their leaves and the roots will therefore not be taking water from the pot. These trees can be placed in a sheltered location while they do not have any leaves on them. They should be placed outside again in time for the new buds to grow in late winter.

Some coniferous trees will not like excessive rain. These varieties should be sheltered from rain, but they still require good light levels.

In general, a good, free-draining soil is best for the autumn and winter weather, which allows the soil to remain moist only throughout the colder months; during spring and summer, you may need to water them more often and even give them a good drenching. If drenching leads to soil splashing off the top of your pot, brush the soil back over and top it up.

I don't want to alarm you but, with some species, if you don't water them for two or three days, then it is highly likely the tree will be damaged irreparably and may even die. When you're thinking about water and your precious bonsai, it is always better to be safe than sorry.

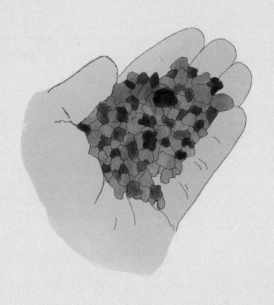

*'A man who asks is a fool for five minutes.
A man who never asks is a fool for life.'*

Your bonsai may live in the most perfect, beautiful pot, with healthy soil, appropriate watering and in an ideal location. You may have put all those elements in place so that your tree has the best chance of thriving and living its best life. There is one more kind act that you can perform to give your tree the greatest chance to be the best version of itself: fertilizer.

Fertilizer provides a bonsai with nutrients and the feed that it needs for future growth. Besides water and oxygen, the roots of a bonsai tree need to take up fertilizer so the tree can remain healthy and maintain its balance. If no fertilizer is added to the soil, the tree will become slower and slower-growing, lose colour, and — eventually — begin to die.

FERTILIZER IS TO BONSAI WHAT LEARNING IS TO PEOPLE.

We need to keep our outlook on life balanced, fresh and healthy by taking in new skills and ideas to enrich ourselves. Just like a nutrient-starved tree, we need new input, new skills and new ideas in order to grow. This might be something small like taking up a stimulating hobby, or considerably bigger, such as learning a second language. And much as the fertilizer applied to a bonsai tree must have meaning and purpose, so too must the learning we take in. Fertilizer has three components — nitrogen, phosphorus and potassium.

Likewise, there are three distinct elements of our life that benefit from learning:

BODY   **MIND**   **SOUL**

Just as with bonsai, you need to regularly feed these three elements with beneficial and nutrient-rich 'fertilizer'; otherwise, your life will stagnate.

Looking at each of these three aspects that require regular 'feeding', we can begin with the simple truth about exercising your body, your 'trunk'. You may eat well, but if you don't exercise regularly, then your body will not be in tip-top condition. How you choose to exercise is up to you; it could be getting up early for a walk, taking up a yoga class or swimming lessons. Maybe going to the gym after work or during your lunch break. You don't need to be Usain Bolt or Arnold Schwarzenegger or break personal bests, but you do need to set a routine that gets you moving.

Next up is learning for the mind. This could be a college course, a book club, or in fact any new learning or skill that starts getting the old grey matter going.

Last but not least is the soul, and this aspect of learning is primarily about yourself, which is a never-ending lesson. For this, we need interaction and socialization. Arrange a meal with friends once a week or catch up over a coffee, even if it's just for ten minutes. Reading self-help books, listening to podcasts or watching inspirational videos are all easily accessible ways to ask yourself questions and explore ideas about your mind and soul — learning how you react in certain circumstances, and even what things are most important to you.

Fertilizer such as this will allow you to re-evaluate the person that you want to be and move forward in your life, just as the right fertilizer will ensure that your bonsai remains healthy, hungry for life and growing enthusiastically.

These three elements that need 'feeding' with the fertilizer of learning are all interlinked; they are balanced with each other — just as your bonsai's trunk, leaves, soil and pot are inextricably connected. Once you start to fertilize your life, you will find that you start to enjoy the process and, before you know it, you are reading more books or regularly analysing where you are in your life. This is because you have opened your mind to learning and improving – just as a healthy bonsai tree will gratefully soak up fertilizer and flourish, your own life can only be enriched by a constant hunger to learn.

I was, and still am, a somewhat quiet person, but back when I was young this was principally down to a lack of confidence. I used to be pretty reserved, and I knew this was holding me back. So I decided to push myself out of my comfort zone and, at the age of twenty-two, I enrolled on a health and fitness instructors' course that led to a diploma. I had a fear of standing up in front of people and being around large numbers, and that is why I decided to face that fear head on and enroll. The truth is, everyone on the course was being pushed out of their comfort zone, yet the support among the students was fantastic.

That diploma was such a rewarding experience and it taught me so much that went way beyond the specifics of the course. I learned how to put together an aerobics routine to music, all choreographed to be on time, including warm-ups and cool-downs; I had to get my head around the physiology of the classes, to ensure I was looking after the attendees and helping them avoid injury; I had to learn to have enough confidence to welcome a room full of adults, all arriving excitedly and expectantly for my class, and then conduct that class confidently, with humour and expertise.

However, that course also allowed me to prove to myself that I could lead people from the front, that I could get people doing what I needed them to do, while making sure they gained plenty of personal benefit themselves. All these lessons remain great personal qualities I am proud to have developed — and, in fact, they later sparked my career move towards management.

Importantly, by grasping the nettle and doing that course, I had enriched, fed, fertilized all three areas of my life that need looking after — my body (obviously), but also my mind, with the learning and study, and my spiritual health, in terms of learning about myself and moving forward with challenges and in areas that I wished to improve upon.

Bonsai has undoubtedly taught me more than any other element in my life. In fact, its impact in terms of enriching and fertilizing my life has been vast.

Different bonsai need different fertilizers, and we are no different — what enriches one person's life won't work for someone else. Just like our bonsai, we are all unique.

Regardless of what subject you want to learn about, we live in an age where learning tools are at our fingertips, so there really is no reason why you can't learn about anything! The great thing about this informal approach to learning and fertilizing your life is that you can go at your own pace — if you can only find ten minutes a day to sit down, then that's fine, the opportunities are still there.

Just know that, once you start learning, it will spark an explosion of curiosity in your mind, body and soul, and there will be no holding you back! You never know, that hobby might end up being your next career, or even a new business! For example, I never thought that I would own a bonsai nursery. That was all down to my mind being open to learning.

So be bold, find your passion and dive in. You never know where it will lead . . .

STAY CURIOUS, FOLKS.
ALWAYS.

Any species of tree can be a bonsai.

'Learning is a treasure
that will follow its
owner everywhere.'
CHINESE PROVERB

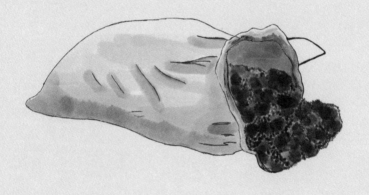

If you want your bonsai to always be healthy and vibrant, it is important that you have a basic grasp of the fertilizers you can use to help them along their way.

Put simply, what you need to know is the make-up of the primary nutrients in the fertilizer, known as the NPK numbers. As mentioned earlier, each letter represents a different nutrient, and each performs a different task for the tree or plant.

Nitrogen (N) is responsible for increasing foliage growth and also for the colour of the foliage. A higher nitrogen content will encourage the tree to put on more top growth.

Phosphorus (P) encourages root development and flowering (if you have a flowering variety) on your tree.

Potassium (K) contributes towards establishing the overall health of the tree, regulating growth of both foliage and roots; it also helps the tree to fight off pests and diseases.

You will see these numbers referenced on packs of fertilizers, for example 'NPK: 5-5-5'. The way they are calculated can be complex but, essentially, the higher the individual number, the higher the amount of that nutrient in the fertilizer. This allows us bonsai keepers to apply a different fertilizer at different times of the year, or to achieve a particular goal in the development of the tree.

For example, we could use a fertilizer with a higher nitrogen value in spring to encourage growth of the tree, then one with a lower nitrogen value towards autumn. A fruiting or flowering tree would require fertilizer with a higher potassium value to encourage flowering and subsequent fruiting to take place.

A key consideration is whether you use chemical or organic fertilizer. At our nursery, we use a slow-release, organic fertilizer that is both reliable and convenient, especially when you have lots of trees to tend to. This fertilizer is placed either in feed baskets or directly on the soil surface, so that when it rains or the trees are watered a little fertilizer dissolves and feeds the tree. When the fertilizer has dissolved, simply add more.

Another consideration would be timing: with deciduous material and conifers in general, a balanced feed from March through to August should do the trick. There is no need for fertilizer during the months of dormancy. For a flowering and fruiting tree, you would apply a higher-potassium feed between March and August. For pines, we do not apply any fertilizer until around late June, at which time the foliage has grown and the fertilizer will not contribute towards larger pine needles (we feed a little later into autumn to compensate).

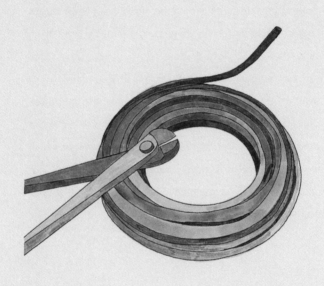

'A closed mind is like a closed book:
just a block of wood.'

Tools are an essential part of nurturing bonsai – we use them to care for, shape and design bonsai so that our trees can remain healthy and, ultimately, hopefully, progress towards where we want them to be.

There are many occasions when we will need these tools. Once most bonsai trees have developed their foliage, there will come a time when those leaves cut out light from the middle of the tree and the central section starts to die out. When we prune it with bonsai tools, the tree can revitalize itself from the inside out and enjoy a new life where, previously, there was no growth.

Similarly, we are lucky to have many 'tools' in our lives that we can use to take care of ourselves and our health, to encourage growth as well as to design our future. Just as a bonsai grower prunes the branches to encourage the tree's growth, our pastimes and hobbies enrich our lives, along with wellbeing techniques such as mindfulness and meditation.

First up, though, a very simple question:

Do you actually have any hobbies?

How many busy people have you met who say, 'I'm too busy for hobbies,' or 'I don't really feel like starting anything new.'

This is not only a great shame, it is also a risk to our health and wellbeing. How can you live a balanced life if you have no pastimes or passions other than work?

Modern life can present many dangers, and it is fair to say that stress, anxiety and burn-out can sometimes seem endemic. So, how can we hope to protect ourselves from these potential risks if we never give ourselves a chance? If you are stressed because all you ever seem to do is work, then, without a hobby or a pastime to distract you and enrich your life, how is that going to change?

The art of pruning or watering a bonsai can be immensely relaxing, just as having the right tools in your life in the form of hobbies and pastimes can be. This way, you can prune out the stresses of your life and replace the areas of your experience that are unfulfilling or unrewarding with exciting new shoots of growth and energy.

Now that you are on the path to being more bonsai, you should think about what hobbies or pastimes you can either continue, re-ignite or start from scratch that will help you achieve the same level of peaceful calmness and relaxation that bonsai allows me.

There is no real secret or tip here, you need to find what feels attractive to yourself. Whether it is a crossword, DIY or paragliding, if it helps you escape, relax and not think about the stresses and strains of the day, then don't view that hobby as a 'nice' part of your life that you want to fit in . . . view it as essential.

Just as we need to perform maintenance to keep our bonsai tools in top shape, we shouldn't be afraid to re-evaluate our relaxation 'tools' from time to time. If your hobby becomes a little boring, repetitive or too demanding, then look to change things up; otherwise, you risk losing the life-enhancing benefits a fulfilling hobby can bring. Likewise, if this maintenance is not carried out on our bonsai tools, they will become blunt and cause more damage than good to the bonsai.

A problem can arise if the hobby you take up to reduce stress and anxiety becomes another source of stress and anxiety. As an example, a good friend of mine was quite stressed about the condition of one of her trees. She explained, clearly quite exasperated, that she was thinking of selling the tree as she could not fix one problematic area of its canopy. I gently pointed out that it simply needed time to fill out and in another year or so the problem would solve itself.

Perfectionism was holding her back and causing stress when in fact the hobby should have been relieving it. The key with any bonsai — and indeed any hobby — is to only work in 'the now' and to enjoy the pastime for what it is, a source of stress relief, never of stress itself.

One of my favourite pastimes is watering the trees at the nursery. I find this time, spending a few moments with each tree, thinking about their health, future development and design, very calming. For me, many tasks within bonsai are an opportunity for mindfulness, and certainly watering is an escape rather than just a chore.

Hopefully, after reading *Be More Bonsai*, caring for tiny trees may become your new hobby. If so, you will be equipped with a new tool that will enrich your life and provide a rewarding distraction from life's stresses and strains. If not, don't worry. Like the tools for your bonsai, it is crucial that you find your own relaxation tools that will work for you, ones that you will enjoy and which will help you find balance.

Although I should add, whenever I am faced with the choice between bonsai and paragliding, I know which one I am going to choose!

To a bonsai beginner, the variety and cost of the many tools available can make the hobby seem very daunting and potentially expensive. Believe it or not, some bonsai scissors can cost as much as $35,000! — they're made as functional miniature works of art by people with a long heritage of crafting only the very finest, elite tools.

However, don't panic!

You can get yourself a set of essential tools much more cheaply.

Bear in mind the old adage, 'Buy well, buy once.' There are very cheap tools out there, but I would always advise to buy the best quality your budget can stretch to.

To begin with, you most definitely need a pair of scissors. It doesn't matter if they are kitchen or hairdressing scissors, they will initially be good enough to have a go at a rudimentary level. When you decide to upgrade, you can buy general bonsai scissors, which can cut both roots and the top foliage. They combine the slightly more robust cutting blades of root scissors with the reach of twig scissors. These are the scissors I personally carry around most of the time – and the ones that end up cutting holes in the back pocket of my jeans.

Branch cutters

Branch cutters have a curved cutting blade that slices a straight but concave cut and are typically used to remove a branch from the trunk. The point of this tool is that the resultant cut will, with time, heal over to be flush with the surrounding area and therefore be better disguised.

Wire cutters

The imaginatively named 'wire cutters' are used . . . to cut wire, but the special thing about these particular bonsai tools comes when you are removing wire from a tree. The rounded head allows you to get right up to the branch while the cutting blades do not pinch the cut wire into the tree.

Jin pliers

No, not that kind of gin! *Jin* is a Japanese term for a branch that has had the bark stripped off and has usually been bleached with lime sulphur. Jin pliers are usually used to crush the bark and strip the branch in order to make jin. They are also useful for twisting and tightening wires.

Chopsticks

Hopefully a free tool from a local fast food restaurant, a chopstick is great for ensuring that soil is filled in around the tree roots during repotting, preventing the air gaps and root dieback that can otherwise result.

Another thing to consider is whether to choose black carbon or stainless-steel tools. Carbon steel will hold its cutting edge longer but it is susceptible to rust and more brittle; with stainless steel, on the other hand, the edge will need sharpening more often, but it is resistant to rust and less brittle, so if you have a habit of leaving tools outside in the rain, then stainless steel it is!

After each use, you should wipe down your tools with an anti-bacterial spray to avoid cross-contamination. You should also undertake regular maintenance of your chosen tools a couple of times a year. Clean the blades to remove old sap, dry them and apply a light finish of oil to lubricate and protect them. This action becomes part of the ritual of bonsai and, in turn, allows you to reap the wellbeing benefits of bonsai.

If your tools become blunted, use a whetstone to sharpen the cutting edge of the blade. Luckily, it takes just a few minutes and needs to be done only once in a while.

'The future depends on what you do today.'

It takes a lot of practice to perfect the wiring of a bonsai tree — in terms of how you apply it, when to do it and how long to leave the wire on. Essentially, the wire is there to support a branch's positioning and is applied for a specific length of time. This allows that positioning to become permanent, or at least as much as nature allows. That in turn causes the bonsai to be shaped and designed in a way that the owner prefers. This wiring takes time and will be repeated often during a bonsai's lifetime, sometimes with a subtle re-shaping, sometimes with something more radical. The crucial skill of wiring is instrumental to the art of bonsai.

We can liken the wiring of a bonsai to your work or your career. Just as wiring supports and redirects a branch, our work or career supports the direction of our life, often allowing a transition between one phase and another – if done correctly, as with wiring, your career and job choices will help you shape your life and achieve your goals.

In bonsai, there are dangers when wiring a tree: over-wiring can strangle the tree, while leaving the wire on too long will result in scars to the branch. We often need to remove wires to prevent them cutting into branches as the tree grows, only to replace the wiring as the chosen branch placement has not yet been set.

Your work is no different.

Certainly, overwork is damaging to our physical and mental wellbeing, and we can quickly develop scars when our work–life balance is not what it should be.

Obviously, this can be avoided if you enjoy your job. The old saying, 'If you enjoy your job, you will never work a day in your life,' is very true – this is when your wiring and your goals are in perfect sync.

Not all of us are lucky enough to be in this position, but if you are able to both practically and financially, you would do well to 're-wire' and change direction if you feel unhappy with the way your career and goals are shaping up.

Think about this simple bit of maths: if you assume that you work from approximately twenty years of age until sixty-five but really do not enjoy the five days a week when you are working, then in very simplified terms and allowing for annual holidays, that 'living for the weekend' approach means you are not enjoying well over two thousand working weeks of your life. That's over ten thousand days.

The wire is a transitional phase for the bonsai, and so should work be for us. Work should not exclusively define who we are. It is amazing how often one of the first questions that crops up when we are introduced to somebody new is 'What do you do?' I find that to be one of the less interesting things about modern society. Instead, I like to ask, 'What are your hobbies or passions?', which results in a far more interesting conversation.

These days, people have multiple jobs and careers over the course of their life, so there does seem to be plenty of opportunity for change, for shaping where you are heading, for re-wiring your career. Certainly, if you don't re-wire at all, then your career will take whatever shape and form it wants to naturally. Sometimes it will still end up in a beautiful place, but often that isn't the case and, in either situation, you will have no control over its direction.

If circumstances allow, don't be afraid to re-wire your tree. Think about how you want your future career to be shaped and you might just surprise yourself!

Wiring is very much a skill that needs to be practised in order for it to be perfected. You can read books and articles or watch the countless videos on the subject, but in order to get the hang of wiring and its intricacies, you need to just start and have a go yourself.

We typically apply wire to a bonsai in autumn, which allows the wire to set over the colder months, then remove it in spring as the tree starts to grow again.

Bonsai wire is available in two variants: copper and aluminium. For beginners, I would recommend aluminium, as it is easier to put on your bonsai and, indeed, to take off. Copper is stiffer and, while it does have certain benefits, which we will come to shortly, it is more difficult to reposition and take off.

When wiring a tree, you will need to gauge how thick a wire you need to use: too thin and the wire will not hold the branch; too thick and the branch will bend around the wire. As a guide, with aluminium you should aim for a wire that is approximately half the diameter of the branch. In order to get the best result, you should aim to apply the wire at an angle of forty-five degrees to the branch but, to begin with, anything between forty-five and sixty degrees will suffice.

Conventional advice is to remove the wire by cutting it away from the tree rather than unwinding it, which can potentially cause damage to the branch. If the bonsai is mature and refined, then cut the wire away to prevent possible damage. (Re-use the wire whenever possible/suitable.)

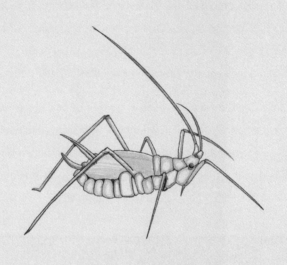

'Treat others as you would be treated.
Devote yourself to that, for there's no
more direct approach to humanity.'

Bonsai owners can become fanatical about scouring their trees for pests and destroying any infestation they find. However, not all insects are bad for a tree, and knowing the difference will be hugely beneficial to the health and wellbeing of your tree — and to you. With your tree and in your life, you need to be able to sort out the baddies from the goodies and take appropriate action.

There are many types of pests that may attack your bonsai and it is very important to understand just how insidious these baddies can be.

These pests will literally suck the life out of your bonsai!

They take away its vigour, its healthy constitution and introduce a lot of toxic stress to the tree. Sometimes pests will almost completely coat a tree and, at that point, they are very much in control, rather than you or the bonsai. For example, when you see an aphid on a bonsai, you might initially spot only one or two. However, if you do not take prompt action, within a week or so, your tree will be swamped by a major infestation.

By contrast, you also need to be aware that there are some insects that are actually very beneficial and help us to get rid of the baddies. We only resort to pesticides as a very last resort, if nature – in the form of beneficial insects and other bug-predators – cannot find a way to assist (usually if we have left it too late).

If you don't stay alert to pests, before you know it, getting rid of them can be incredibly challenging.

The pests we face in our everyday lives are people who are a negative presence. This can be for a number of reasons – perhaps they are struggling with their own challenges, or following some agenda that you are unaware of. Like pests around your bonsai, our own pests present significant risks to our physical health, our way of living and our mental wellbeing. Whatever the reason for these 'pests' being in your life, you need to be alert and take appropriate action when you spot a problem.

So, what do I mean by pests in our lives? Thankfully, human pests aren't as many and varied as their insect equivalents; nonetheless, they can be just as damaging. Here are the three main culprits that can prove toxic to your wellbeing:

1. 'EMOTIONAL APHIDS' literally suck the pure life out of you and leave you feeling emotionally and physically exhausted. These are people for whom nothing is ever good enough, and they complain constantly and have a tendency to make their problems your problems. What's more, they are never thankful for any help or support you give them and they never offer help or support in return. Often you are left wondering why you bothered to become their friend or acquaintance in the first place.

2. 'PEST-IMISTS' can put a negative spin on even the most exciting or positive of situations, and once they've made their cynical remarks, it is often very hard to put these unhelpful thoughts out of your mind.

3. 'WHINE WEEVILS' may not necessarily fall into either of the first two categories, but when you talk to them

about an idea or plan, they only tell you the reasons why you can't or shouldn't do something.

Maybe you've read through these descriptions and recognize some of these behaviours in people around you — or in yourself. You may realize that, in some situations, you are your own pest. The good news is that you are in control of whatever pests you find in your life and, once you spot them, you can take action.

You can take a three-stage approach towards tackling these pests.

Let's start by taking a good look at yourself to see if you recognize any of these traits in the way you behave towards yourself.

You should be your own best friend.

You should be positive and encouraging towards yourself, and proud of your uniqueness. Unfortunately, many of us struggle to feel that way, and this lack of confidence can be a real burden in life. I know people who are brilliantly helpful, supportive and positive with their friends and family but don't exhibit these wonderful behaviours with themselves . . . and that is a real shame.

I know a writer who, when he was just starting out and had only published one book, was explaining to a fellow author how he would have written his debut differently, how this paragraph in the text wasn't right and that chapter wasn't ideal, despite this first book having done extremely well and proven to be very popular. The more seasoned writer asked him, 'Why do you give yourself a bad review? There are so many people out there who will do that for you – don't do that yourself!'

Similarly, are you your own worst enemy?

Also, do you perhaps suffer from 'imposter syndrome'? You know your own ability, you have already 'walked the walk', but you still feel that you are not fully developed enough to be considered an authority on a certain subject. This can work to undermine your confidence in your own ability and stop you from pushing forward. Just remember that there is always more you could know but, equally, there are many people out there who may be eager to benefit from what you already know.

If you recognize this type of 'pest in the mirror', then flip all this around and become your own number-one fan!

Be kinder to yourself.

From today, stop writing your own bad reviews.

While you are looking in the mirror, make an honest appraisal of how you behave towards others.

Is it possible that you are the pest in someone else's life?

Are you cynical when they talk to you about their day or something they are excited about? Do you look for the negative in the situations of others? Give some thought to why you might sometimes behave in this way and how you can change your outlook to offer a more supportive outlook.

Whenever you can, offer simple words of encouragement. It rarely takes more than 'You can do it' or 'I'm sure you'll figure it out' or 'That sounds like a fantastic idea.' When you offer this positive support, often, you will see the other person's face light up, and that may be because you are the first person who has actually listened to them and then encouraged them. Think and say 'Why not?' more often than 'No chance'. If the answer really should be a no, then don't just flatly answer in the negative but try to explain why it's currently a no and consider potential alternatives or work-arounds.

It's time for your first ever 'Sponsored Bug-blast Day'.

Choose a day next week – preferably sooner rather than later – and spend the ENTIRE day ONLY giving positive opinions, praise and ideas. Make a conscious effort, as if you were being sponsored to do it.

Don't allow ONE SINGLE negative comment or thought to come from you. This applies both to yourself and towards others. Focus really hard on doing this all day . . . you are being 'sponsored', remember?

When you see or read the news on your Sponsored Bug-blast Day, don't just tut or shake your head. If you find the news impossible to stay positive about, then don't watch it. You wouldn't eat a burger and chips on the day of a sponsored run, so don't do the equivalent on your Sponsored Bug-blast Day.

Who else do you talk to in your day that you could be exclusively positive with? Look for chances to support, compliment or genuinely offer a little of your time.

Once you've done your Sponsored Bug-blast Day, first, pat yourself on the back, and then have a good, honest look at how you did.

If it were a running race, would you have finished?

Would you feel comfortable collecting your sponsorship money?

Hopefully, you will have been very pleasantly surprised at how good this day of exclusive positivity feels . . . both for you personally and from the reactions of those around you. Then think about making this commitment a permanent change — just as some 'sponsored fun runners' enjoy their first race so much they become life-long marathon competitors.

This third type of pest in our lives is a little trickier to deal with, because we are talking about people who undermine your wellbeing and happiness. Are you surrounded by people who genuinely have your health and wellbeing at heart, or are some of them causing you more problems than they are solving? It's not always easy to move away from people you sense might be toxic, or at least unhelpful, but it is vital for your mental wellbeing that you do so.

The mind coach and author Don Macpherson gives one example of a famous motor-racing driver who had come through the ranks with his dad by his side — but when he got to the big leagues, his dad would always be with him on the grid, and the last thing he'd say as the engines were turned on ready to race was, 'Don't crash!' Eventually, this particular driver got the courage to tell his well-meaning but ultimately unhelpful father to keep away from the grid so close to the start of the race.

If you spot negative and unhelpful behaviours in others around you, whether it's colleagues, family or friends, you have some very important decisions to make. Be aware of how they react when you talk to them: are they encouraging you and enriching your life, or are they nibbling away at your roots?

If this person is an acquaintance, then you should grasp the nettle and stop being around that particular pest. If they are a closer friend, you still need to be honest and exercise self-care by asking yourself, 'Is my life better for having this person in it?' This can extend to technology, not just personal interactions. For example, when your phone rings, do you sometimes see a name flash up on the screen and think, *Oh, no, what are they going to want?* If your heart sinks when a certain person calls, then maybe think about how much longer that pest should be in your life.

Bad relationships drain the energy and health from us. If you have relationships that are emotionally exhausting, that zap the energy from you, leaving you physically or mentally fatigued, you have to ask yourself, 'Is this person going to change or do I need to take action?' Expecting people to change is not always realistic – but they must want to change if they value you. I appreciate that some pests can't be removed from your life so easily. If that is the case, then you should try to control the amount of time you spend with these people or, when you are with them, steer away from talking about any issues that might prompt their negative behaviour.

Sadly, some people will always be a pest, but that doesn't mean you have to always be around them.

Have perspective on your pest control – remember, locking yourself away to avoid pests may also keep your positive, beneficial friends away – like our helpful insects on the bonsai leaf. When we look for change or to accomplish things, we need people that support us. Having the support of family and friends is crucial to help you keep going when you really feel like giving up.

Do you want to spend your time in a nursery full of healthy, vibrant trees with no infestations, or do you want to knowingly go to a place where there are bugs coming out of every crevice? Seek to fill your life with people who are positive about your choices and are willing to help you along the way.

Now you know the type of pests that can eat away at your roots, you can eradicate or at least limit any damage before it happens. And once you have removed the pests from your life, learn from bonsai and be patient with yourself — always understand that if a caterpillar eats a leaf, you can remove the problem, but you also need the patience to let the leaf return to its former glory.

Don't spend your day avoiding sap-sucking pests when you could be surrounded by beautiful and beneficial insects.

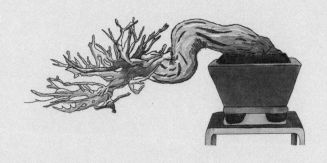

'The best time to plant a tree was twenty years ago.
The second-best time is now.'

A customer walked into the nursery one day, held out his hand to shake mine, smiled slightly nervously and said, 'I am relying on you to save my marriage.' Now, customers often ask me unusual questions or tell me surprising things when we initially meet, but this was a first.

No pressure!

It turned out that he had left it to the very last minute to find his wife a birthday present. He explained that even though his wife was known for not liking, or even remotely enjoying, gardening, for some reason he had decided that a bonsai would be an ideal gift. Knowing very little about bonsai himself, he had kept putting the task off, until, in a last-minute panic, he had hastily charged around all the local garden centres, desperately attempting to find a nice starter tree.

The problem was, it was now five o'clock on a Saturday evening and the shops were closing soon, so the only 'bonsai' he had been able to find was in very poor condition on a dusty shelf in one garden centre. By his own admission, it looked 'like a stubby old root'. He added, in a somewhat desperate tone, 'I can't give that to my wife – it's a disgrace.'

To be fair, I didn't see that ending well for him! Sold as an indoor bonsai, the ficus was struggling to stay alive, not least because it was housed in a glass pot with no drainage, effectively meaning it was rotting from the roots up.

'OK,' I said, after his 'save my marriage' introduction, 'let's see what we can do . . . '

We walked around the nursery and talked about bonsai types, style and maintenance issues, and his budget, and he eventually picked a nice, slightly wonky juniper tree, principally because it looked like his wife's favourite tree near where they lived. He immediately relaxed and I could see that his panic was subsiding.

'When is it your wife's birthday?' I asked, keen to know how close he had run this to the wire.

'Er, today!'

I can report that the last-minute birthday present was very well received, the marriage was saved and, in fact, his family have since become very good customers. However, that rather agitated and frantic episode did remind me of one element of bonsai that I use in almost every aspect of my daily life: planning.

You can't rush a bonsai.

We know what seasons are coming and what tasks each time of the year brings for bonsai. You can't decide to repot a bonsai sooner than you should, as it might adversely impact its health, and missing the repotting window means that it will have to wait another year. We know when to start fertilizing and when to stop. We know when to wire trees for shaping and when not to. We know when deciduous trees will drop their leaves. If you are exhibiting a bonsai, you can't wait until the morning of a competition and hastily chop away at the leaves in the vain hope that it will suddenly look good.

Just like birthdays, all these things need an element of planning.

In short, most elements of looking after bonsai are predictable, give or take a few weeks. Yet I see people all the time who are stressing about their trees or rushing around trying to find tools or soil, food or pots, all very last minute. Like that errant husband with his last-minute birthday present.

For all the jokes, this customer was actually pretty stressed when he arrived at the nursery. He loved his wife and didn't want her to think he hadn't made an effort.

My simple approach is to take a time slot, usually during December or January, to plan key forthcoming bonsai events. Check your own stocks of wire, soils and identify the trees you plan to repot. You can then take a few weeks to find the perfect pot and any other items you need. Buying early and being in possession of the required items certainly helps to reduce panic situations.

Much the same applies to life's predictable and repeatable events, birthdays included. We all need to find our own methods of planning for tasks, events and occasions. One very simple idea is to set an alert on your phone the month before, then that will give you time to start looking around for information. If it is a bonsai tree you are after, find a couple of local nurseries, visit them, see what they have ... it sounds so easy and obvious and it is, but for this particular customer even this most simple and potentially very enjoyable of tasks had turned into a whirlwind of panic and rushing about, just because of a lack of planning. It's obviously quite useful to plan ahead for major events, but bonsai has taught me that planning the small moments can really help to smooth out life's ruffles too.

Life has a habit of throwing us curveballs, and forward-planning can help to reduce the impact these have on the bigger picture. It's just like adding in a little extra travel time to easily accommodate any unforeseen traffic jams, pit stops or a flat tyre. If a journey takes an hour, try to allow at least seventy-five or, preferably, ninety minutes. Ideally half as much again, if practical. A friend of mine calls this the 'fudge factor' – and this simple habit means that he is very rarely late and is much calmer when he arrives after a relaxed and peaceful journey.

So, go on, plot out your week, month or even year ahead – plan when you intend to do things, make the most of the technology we all have at our fingertips to help remind you, and turn what can be stressful, rushed experiences into enjoyable, calm and rewarding ones.

Don't be that person who finds themselves in a garden centre at closing time buying a stubby old root!

'When the finger points to the moon,

the imbecile looks at the finger.'

'To know the road ahead, ask those coming back.'

There is a ficus bonsai in Crespi, Italy, that is over a thousand years old; and there is an old juniper bonsai in Mansei-en in Japan that is a similar age. These trees are rare but not entirely an exception — there are plenty of examples of celebrated bonsai that are many hundreds of years old.

In general, age in bonsai is celebrated and venerated. Often, a gnarly or twisted trunk is prized. Thicker trunks that taper naturally can only be created over time and are also cherished. There are short-cuts that people take, but authentic aged trunks can only be a glorious consequence of a life well lived. The same goes for pots — the older examples are effectively artefacts more than just antiques and are treated with appropriate reverence.

If you have visited a bonsai nursery, I bet that the first question you asked might have been, 'How old is this tree?' I am asked this all the time by customers; either that or 'What is the oldest tree you have here?' People directly assign the age of a bonsai with its perceived value, or vice versa. Yet in life we seem to do the opposite. Older people are often treated with much less respect for the simple fact that they are old. A friend of mine has an acquaintance in the computer world who was told – at the age of forty-two – that he was 'past a viable point' to continue working at a certain technology company. This is despite this man having worked in that trade since he was nineteen and having over two decades of experience.

Older people often face problems like this, yet if you think about it, they are simply being penalized for living a long life. If we are being more bonsai, we should prize those more characterful 'trunks' and understand that we can learn from their experience, listen to their stories and wonder at the many years of events that they have witnessed.

'The present moment
is the only time over which
we have dominion.'

THICH NHAT HANH

However, in contrast, this much emphasis on the importance of age in bonsai is unnecessary. There are fifty-year-old trees that look terrible and could barely be called a bonsai; there are also trees probably less than a decade old that look fantastic. Just like going to an art gallery, you may like one painting but not another — the age of either is not a factor. Bonsai is art and should be judged on that basis, not just on age. The only things that matter are the health of the bonsai and whether or not the person buying, or simply looking at, the tree likes it.

However, be open to embracing an older bonsai tree's wrinkles: learn from the tree, admire the seasons that it has seen come and go and always treat the older tree with the respect and decency it deserves.

While we are on the subject of age, we need to talk about time . . .

Every bonsai owner has to accept that their tree may well outlive them. As the Chinese proverb says, 'It is a wise person that plants a tree knowing they will never sit in its shade.'

The longevity of bonsai is complemented by an absence of

haste. The faster the progression on a bonsai tree, the more stress the tree is likely to be placed under. You will often hear bonsai artists talking about a decade here, fifteen years there, and see people outside bonsai circles shaking their heads in disbelief at such elongated time-frames. OK, so I'm not suggesting you put off that overdue DIY project for another decade, but we would do well to learn from bonsai's serene, slow, graceful approach to life. Modern life is the exact opposite to bonsai's gentler pace. Speed is celebrated – same-day delivery, next-day returns, fast food, fast fashion, faster broadband, 'making a quick buck'. A weekend edition of *The New York Times* presents us with more information than a thirteenth-century person would have been exposed to in a lifetime. That's a quick way to get a lifetime of learning!

Society seems to be constantly speeding.

If this faster pace of life is so essential, how come many of us feel that we are never moving fast enough?

Why do we feel that we never have enough time?

Why the rush?

Life doesn't have to be that way.

In these times of such fast-paced, relentless lifestyles, people can all too easily feel stressed and overwhelmed. When we adopt a calm, slower approach – when we are more bonsai – we can blossom.

More than anything, bonsai teaches you to live in the 'now'. When you are shaping and pruning a tree with your scissors, your problems can often be put into sharp perspective.

All you can do is work on the tree that you have in front of you now.

It is about the task, not the outcome.

Take your time.

For me, working on bonsai is my favourite mindfulness activity. I can shut out everything and just focus on what is in front of me: that tiny little tree. When we are pruning a bonsai, it requires our full focus to realize the desired design. There is little point attempting to prune a bonsai when you are thinking about something else, and certainly not while you are angry or frustrated. One young customer in his late teens came to me at the nursery one day and said he'd badly pruned one of his trees because he'd had a stressful day with work and had come home, his mind still distracted – then he went and pruned his bonsai, which was effectively 'caught in the crossfire' of his intense day.

The same applies when we come home from work and perhaps shout at the kids over something and nothing – it's not their fault that your boss is a pain or that a deadline is too rushed, any more than it is the bonsai's fault. Imagine taking your pruning scissors to your bonsai and, as you clip away frantically, shouting, 'Don't do that!' or 'This is all I need after the day I've had!'

You wouldn't, would you?

In these moments, instead of 'taking it out' on our bonsai or on the loved ones around us, we would do well to take a deep breath and do the exact opposite – pruning bonsai can help all those stresses subside, just as playing with your kids or sitting down for a catch-up with your partner can ease the stresses and strains of the day.

Focus on what *truly matters*.

It's not always easy, of course. There are many distractions in modern life, all fighting for our attention. Mobile phones, for instance, are a great invention, but they also intrude on our focus. Text messages, emails, social media notifications – the list of instant interruptions is endless, and we are all guilty of allowing it. I turn on the 'do not disturb' mode on my mobile phone and time it to start and finish twice a day to allow me some time to focus on things of importance.

Better still, get in the habit of turning your phone off altogether.

At the end of the day, if someone is important to you, then they deserve your full attention and you need to find ways to give them that.

You can learn to apply this focus to many of your daily activities, too, so that they can become a mindfulness activity in themselves. It might not be bonsai, it could be gardening, walking the dog or working around the house. The opportunities to step back from the noise and chatter and just focus are there if you look for them.

What – or *who* – deserves your full focus?

Enjoy the fact the tree – and your life – looks good today . . . it will change soon enough but, for now, enjoy where it is at this moment.

Some days a bonsai doesn't need any attention; likewise, you need to learn to have time when you don't do anything, you just relax and enjoy the 'now'. A bonsai is a process, a journey, not just an end goal.

Happiness is the same.

A bonsai is always growing, progressing and evolving. It cannot and should never be rushed. Nor should you.

There are several indicators of age on a bonsai tree, although it is worth noting that it is very difficult to verify an exact age. Ultimately, you cannot accurately judge a tree's age without cutting it in half and counting the rings. I certainly wouldn't allow that anyway, but the real question is: does it really matter?

The first method of ascertaining a tree's age would be the size of the tree and, in particular, the girth of the trunk. It can be a common misconception that the thicker the trunk, the older the tree. This is correct to a degree, but age can be expedited.

A telltale factor when somebody has tried to mimic age in a trunk is what is known as 'trunk chop', which is, quite literally, taking a short cut. The tree is allowed to grow taller to create the desired thickness of trunk, then cut down to height, and a new branch structure and canopy is grown. This cut is hard to disguise and cover up.

Instead, you should look for a visible taper along the length of the trunk, as this is something that only comes as a result of years of steady work. We therefore look for a good-sized trunk with a clear, natural taper as it moves upwards.

Alternatively, we could carve the chopped area to look like a natural feature, having been battered by the elements over its lifetime. This takes skill to perfect, but you would still presume that a considerable trunk chop had been done.

We can also look at the bark of the tree as an indicator of age. People develop wrinkles with age, and to some degree trees are the same. When they are young, the bark is smooth, but as the tree gets older, its bark develops species-related characteristics. A pine tree will become scale-like with flaky bark, while an oak will develop fissures; there are maples that will develop a pine bark effect with age. A Scots pine will become craggy and more wrinkled as it ages. Its bark is similar to the wrinkles on our skin but, unlike us, bonsai culture heralds these signs of age – they are indicators of the passing of time and experience and they are coveted as such. Likewise, if a bonsai tree is badly looked after, the appearance will be noticeably affected, with rotting bark and visible patches of ill health on the tree.

The age of a bonsai does garner value in terms of how long it has been cared for and developed, but don't let that be your only guide as to how much the tree in front of you is to be prized.

A Japanese white pine that was born in 1625 survived the atomic bombing of Hiroshima, protected by a walled garden, despite being only two miles from the epicentre of the explosion.

'*No one can make you feel inferior*
without your consent.'
Eleanor Roosevelt

Welcome to my most hypocritical chapter — this is the one where I give you my opinion that you shouldn't listen to other people's opinions, but hear me out . . .

Bonsai trees come in all sizes, shapes and varieties. Often, I catch a glimpse of a tree I have owned for a long time and suddenly see it in a new light. I might have looked at this particular tree countless times before and moved on, but for some reason it will appear different to me. A bonsai tree is a 360-degree living artwork and, although we assign a 'front' to each tree, it can be viewed from any angle or side. Sometimes, you may prefer the tree looking slightly off-centre; sometimes you may not like the tree whichever side you view it from. The point is that you can constantly review and revise your opinion of a tree depending on which angle you look at it from.

Your opinions of people are the same.

If you have a set opinion of someone and you only ever look at them from the same angle, then it is highly likely that your opinion is never going to change. You might be happy with that stance and, if so, that is up to you — but I would encourage you to always look at people in the same way I feel you should look at the bonsai in my nursery . . . from different perspectives.

When it comes to choosing a bonsai, I always suggest that people turn the trees, tilt them and pick them up in order to get a feel for each one. To form their own opinions.

Always welcome ideas and opinions that are different to yours. In a world of social media and websites feeding us content we 'may like', there is a very real chance that we spend all day, every day, watching, listening and agreeing with the same ideas over and over again. The media term for this is living inside an 'echo chamber', where the ideas and opinions you seek out are merely reflections of your own thoughts.

I understand why people enjoy echo chambers, as they can feel reassuring. There is no challenge, and this perceived endorsement can make a person feel knowledgeable and intelligent. The problem with it is, how are you growing? How are you considering life from different perspectives? Is it really the way to find balance?

I frequently ask customers at the nursery what they think of changes I plan to make to various trees. This allows them to express their thoughts and helps me to take a balanced view of taking that tree forward, without just following my own ideas.

I would also suggest taking this more balanced approach when you meet someone for the first time: always start with a blank page in terms of your opinion of them. You may meet someone a friend has told you all about — good or otherwise. Don't let someone else's opinion cloud your own assessment of that new acquaintance; always start with a blank page. Your friend will have been looking at this person from their own unique perspective, most likely in a different situation and certainly with different background views to yours, so what they think and what you think are unrelated.

In many ways, your opinion of someone else is your problem; the truth is that opinions are only useful to the person who holds them, and they can sometimes become warped and do more harm than good when shared. My opinions of others, and indeed any issues that I have with others, are entirely of my making, and not theirs. If I saw a bonsai that I thought was neglected or ill-treated, I wouldn't walk up to the owner and berate them for the state of the tree; neither will I rush to offer my opinion on someone.

That's just not the bonsai way.

You never know what someone may be going through, or what they are thinking or feeling. They may have had a bad day, or bad week, or a terrible year — so give everyone some slack before forming an opinion about them.

Life can be hard, but judging someone can be harsher.

That said, if your opinion is exclusively nice and positive, then fire away! We all need a little ego boost from time to time, so if you meet someone and think they are fantastic, don't be shy in letting them know. Your kindness will be appreciated and often rewarded. If you can, be kind and thoughtful in your opinions; if not, then do you really need to express your opinion at all?

One final opinion from me about the opinions of others and their opinions of you (feel free to look up 'contradiction in terms' in the dictionary). While we may prefer or even request that people keep their opinions to themselves, they seldom do. Sometimes those opinions come from a place of spite or envy. Regardless of how kind and caring a person is, there are always going to be people who loudly voice their negative opinions.

However, you should always remind yourself that you cannot control those opinions or those people. You may not like what you hear, but those people don't matter to your life. The people who know you and care about you understand the real you, how you operate and how valuable and cherished you are in their lives.

Simply ignore those negative opinions.

They are no more relevant to your life than someone else's view of your bonsai. Giving time to these opinions just adds more wood to the fire. Imagine a bonsai sitting there in a nursery or at a show, faced by a person who is criticizing and picking fault with the little tree in front of them – the bonsai couldn't care less!

Furthermore, you should not alter your behaviour or aspirations simply because of what others may think. Do not be afraid of attempting to do something, or making a particular choice, just because you are concerned about comments from someone else. Don't let other people's opinions clip your wings.

Make sure to always look at a situation from all sides, don't be put off by the opinions of others and, if you like what you see, tell someone!

So be kind, be considerate, be thoughtful . . . and don't forget to look at life from every angle!

'One who is too insistent
on his own views, finds few
to agree with him.'

LAO TZU

Other people's opinions often directly influence how much we pay for many things in life, not just bonsai. So I'm going to preface this section by saying that if a bonsai feels right for you – just as with a car, an item of clothing, jewellery, a house, and so on – and the price feels right to you, go for it!

Now that I have encouraged you to overpay for that old classic car or designer handbag that you simply have to own, back in the world of bonsai, prices can vary hugely, even from one nursery to the next. Starter trees can be bought at many local garden centres for a few pounds, but if you want to buy older, higher-quality trees, you can quickly spend thousands. Since the advent of stricter import/ export regulations, certain trees from specific territories attract higher costs. Many countries operate a strict quarantine system where trees are kept isolated from the native population for long periods of time, often months, before they are allowed to be sold in that territory. Unfortunately, with many countries insisting on the soil being removed, many trees can die during this process, which reduces supply, which, in turn, can increase prices.

However, don't be frightened by cost. Online searches will quickly reveal nearby bonsai nurseries – there are more than you think! – and at these specialist locations you should be getting a tree that is both cared for and high quality. Yes, you will pay a little more, but there is a reason for that. And if you buy a really cheap, neglected tree from a non-specialist which then dies in a few weeks, that will have proven to be a lot more expensive.

The value of a bonsai can be affected by a number of elements, and size is not necessarily the main one. The age of the tree is a certain factor, with anything older than a century almost guaranteed to fetch a high price. The more mature a bonsai appears, the higher the cost usually, although, as I mentioned previously, trees can be 'aged' to look older than they really are.

A thicker trunk will often draw a higher price too but, as I also mentioned earlier, there are methods for making trunks thicker in a relatively short space of time (although this will always leave telltale signs and scarring). Essentially, to reiterate, a genuinely thick trunk that has been grown over many, many years will have a natural taper to it, a feature that cannot be created commercially in a short time. Individual species also differ in price, as some are harder to grow than others.

The ultra-rare trees that are famous around the bonsai world can fetch eye-watering prices. In 2011, the so-called 'Old White Pine' sold for $1.3 million at the Asia-Pacific Bonsai and Suiseki Convention and Exhibition in Japan. There are reports of a 250-year-old juniper bonsai selling for $2 million! Often, these super-rare trees change hands without being in the public domain.

That reminds me, I must check on my savings account . . .

Bon translates as 'tray'; *sai* means 'plant'.

'Better a diamond with a flaw
than a pebble without.'

There is an age-old Chinese story that recounts how, when some people came across the last and only tree standing in a felled forest, the question was asked, 'Why was that tree left standing?'

The answer was that the tree was too twisted and gnarled to be useful. It would not have made good timber for construction and it wasn't conventionally 'attractive' enough to fashion into furniture. Deemed to be useless.

By contrast, in the world of bonsai, uniqueness is celebrated.

Bonsai come in all different shapes, sizes and types — from

the smallest, *mame* ('bean' in Japanese) up to the largest, *imperial* bonsai. These little trees proudly show their age and battle scars from life. Bonsai that are collected in the wild (with the correct permissions) are known as *yamadori* – usually gnarled, twisted and weatherworn, most definitely not straight or 'perfect'. In fact, their 'imperfections' are what make each one individual. Each tree has a unique arrangement of branches, trunk size and shape, and there are endless different idiosyncrasies and a myriad combinations for an individual tree to display its unique properties.

The bonsai grower highlights and nurtures this individuality with pride. There are techniques to create and enhance elements such as 'deadwood' features (*jin* or *shari*). Where a tree has been damaged or perhaps a branch severed, the wound will be left visible, because that event is part of the wonderfully unique life of that particular tree.

Although bonsai growers love to play their part, the most prized trees will have been sculpted by nature over decades or centuries, with no thought to being perfect. From our perspective, we cannot create such innate beauty. That is nature's job.

Well, guess what? Nature made you, too!

Life may have beaten you down, added a few battle scars and knocked your confidence along the way, but the one thing you should always be confident about is being you. Like bonsai, each and every one of us has the gift of uniqueness and, if you think about it . . . just as no two bonsai are the same, no one else can be you.

Unfortunately, we humans do not always follow the same guidelines. Many of us hide away our physical and inner selves so as to avoid being hurt. Modern society places so much value and prestige on appearance, a certain look, the way things 'should be'. Cosmetics, fashion, the media, advertising . . . the notion of appearance is everywhere we look. Often this relentless focus can feel suffocating and intimidating, but if you find yourself feeling pressured, then you need to be more bonsai about it.

There are two elements to this: physical and mental. Starting with the physical, I cannot stress strongly enough that you are what you are, you must not pressure yourself to conform to someone else's ideal. Imagine two prized bonsai trees sitting next to each other – one splendid in its formal upright elegance; the other a gnarly tree, cascading down out of its pot like a green waterfall.

Would one be judged as 'incorrect' simply because it sits next to the other?

Your individuality needs to be celebrated, just as it is in bonsai.

There are endless ways in which we can look different to the next person, so I won't list them all here! Suffice to say, if you like a certain outfit, piercings, tattoos, or none of the above, then great, that is you and that is how you should look. You should also exercise the same attitude towards other people: they need to be how they are, and we must not judge them for that. Don't judge a book by its cover may well be a much-used platitude, but it is with good reason.

The mental side of being unique is equally crucial to your wellbeing. You will never meet someone in life who has exactly the same opinions on every single topic of conversation. As long as those opinions do not hurt, offend or impose on anyone else, then that is a good thing. Your own life experience means that, by definition, you are unique.

No one else has lived your life. As Oscar Wilde put it, 'Be yourself; everyone else is already taken.'

However, in life, we all too often find that differences are the source of tension, stress or ill will. People may feel like an outsider because of how they look, sound or behave. This is unhealthy and not the bonsai way. The goal in bonsai is not to make every tree look the same or to pressure other trees to conform to a certain style; the bonsai way is to strive to make every tree individual and to celebrate its uniqueness.

Once you acknowledge your own 'gnarly' uniqueness and that you are a beautiful *yamadori* one-off, your confidence will blossom. If a lack of confidence is getting in your way, choose to change that. It will take a little effort, patience and sometimes help, but it will be worth it.

We can be almost anything, as long as we have confidence.

We can boost our confidence by recognizing our own uniqueness and working with that, rather than fighting against it . . .

. . . by not being too straight a tree and loving that fact.

'The journey is the reward.'

I am never more at peace and happy than when I am working on, and surrounded by, my bonsai. This tangible, visceral connection with nature can touch us all. This is not just about bonsai — spend any amount of time in a beautifully green space and the benefits to your wellbeing and sense of balance are undeniable.

This is not just a passionate bonsai grower offering a biased view. In 2017, the World Health Organization published a report into 'Urban Green Space Interventions and Health'. The study found that the 'modern urban lifestyle is associated with chronic stress, insufficient physical activity [and] exposure to environmental hazards. Urban green spaces . . . can promote mental and physical health, reduce morbidity and mortality in urban residents by providing psychological relaxation and stress alleviation, stimulating social cohesion, supporting physical activity, and reducing exposure to air pollutants, noise and excessive heat.'

On a daily level, this expert opinion is easily endorsed by taking a gentle stroll through a woodland or park after a stressful day. Essentially, it is the connection with nature that triggers these multiple health benefits. Aside from the air being cleaner, being in nature creates a sense of escape from everyday life, space to reflect and relax.

However, for many people, a country walk is not an option — that may be simply due to where they live, a lack of transport or access to areas of natural greenery. Not all of us are lucky enough to regularly spend quality time in nature. That's where bonsai can come in: your own little slice of serene nature in your home. Whether you have a balcony, a porch, a yard or a garden, you will find a bonsai that is suitable for the space you have. The beauty of bonsai is that they can encapsulate the natural wonder of green spaces and condense that into a manageable amount without losing the pure essence. Plus, you can enrich the benefits of having a bonsai in your own space by letting your imagination run free. If you have a simple, beautiful bonsai, imagine sitting underneath that tree, soaking up nature; if you have bought a landscape of several trees, then picture yourself walking through all those elegant trunks.

A bonsai aims to emulate the same species in real life. In a similar way, it is also a wonderfully rewarding pastime to try to mimic a special tree from childhood. My grandparents had a golden willow tree in their garden. I would walk underneath it, and the trailing branches would create what felt like my own little enclosed, private space. Playing in and around trees as children is an essential part of growing up. Do you fondly recall a particular tree from your childhood that you could mimic with a bonsai?

Modern life's move away from nature has been accelerating at some pace for decades. As more people converge and populate cities, access to green space is reduced, meaning that our own little space becomes increasingly important. This becomes ever more difficult as living in cities becomes more expensive and people live in increasingly costly apartments where the outside space is limited to a balcony or a window ledge. Also, more people than ever now rent property, which often means there is less of a sense of ownership and belonging to a house and/or garden, and modern life is also making so many of us transient, whether it's moving for work, family reasons or as a lifestyle change. However, with bonsai, the magical thing is that our potted friends can come with us anywhere, at a moment's notice. You get to take your green space with you: just pop your bonsai in your car or on public transport and off you go . . . your own little slice of nature, wherever you are.

In such a hectic, compressed world, always remember that these wonderful little trees will provide you with a familiar, calming and stable influence. No matter what is going on in your life, your bonsai will always be there at the end of the day when you come home. It will have been sitting there waiting, it won't judge, it won't pressure or change what it expects of you, it is just being bonsai — calmly, slowly and serenely. Bonsai will gently remind you of life's priorities, help you to take better care of yourself and your loved ones, keep you focused and, ultimately, be alongside you to help you find balance in every corner of your day. There is a very warming and reassuring reliability to that — all they ask for in return is a little watering when needed, some nice food now and again but, above all, for you to lovingly care for and nurture them, to guide them towards their best, balanced life. And hopefully, in doing this, you will achieve the same for yourself.

By being around these tiny pots of wisdom, you can be more bonsai.

They are our companions for life and offer us a lesson in every leaf.

We need bonsai now, more than ever.

So, what are you waiting for?!

See you at the nursery . . .

'A bird does not sing
because it has an answer.
It sings because it has a song.'

ACKNOWLEDGEMENTS

*'Everyone has a book inside
of them — but it doesn't do
any good until you pry it out'*

Jodi Picoult

These words describe me well, so I have to thank the following people for their efforts to not only pry the manuscript out, but also for creating the reality of this printed book.

My biggest thanks go to Martin. This book would certainly not have been possible without the long hours and many lengthy discussions. Martin's dedication allowed my manuscript to be compiled from a collection of thoughts and turned into a cohesive and, hopefully, helpful book.

I thank my wife, Sally, who read through the manuscript at each stage to provide constructive feedback and acted as devil's advocate to make sure each point was clear and understood.

For the images in this book, both photographic and hand drawn, I have to thank Alfie Blue and Korda Ace. Last-minute changes and additions are always stressful, and I thank them for accommodating these requests.

Both gratitude and thanks go out to Penguin Random House, specifically to Dan Bunyard for having faith in the idea of *Be More Bonsai*, and to Paula Flanagan for fabulously undertaking the role of editor.

Finally, my thanks go out to my parents, Carole and Brian, for keeping the nursery running while I was otherwise engaged during the writing of this book.